文化里的中国
CULTURAL CHINA

编 著 张 玫 谭月娥 杜 娟 吴 坤 丁黎明
配 图 陈 晨

中国人民大学出版社
·北京·

序

　　习近平总书记强调，文化是一个民族的魂魄，文化认同是民族团结的根脉。要着眼建设中华民族现代文明，不断构筑中华民族共有精神家园。党的二十大报告强调："讲好中国故事、传播好中国声音，展现可信、可爱、可敬的中国形象。"中华文明是世界上唯一绵延不断且以国家形态发展至今的伟大文明，准确把握中华文明的突出特性，推动文化繁荣、建设文化强国、讲好中国故事和中华民族故事，为铸牢中华民族共同体意识奠定坚实的精神和文化基础，是时代赋予我们的新的文化使命。中华文化的博大精深体现在其悠久的历史和丰富的传统上。充分挖掘中华优秀传统文化元素，利用图书这一讲好中国故事和中华民族故事的重要载体、语言这一传播中国声音的桥梁纽带、互联网这一展现中国形象的有效渠道，让世界了解全方位的、立体的中国，了解中国各民族在长期交往、交流、交融中孕育而成的精神纽带，是北方民族大学张玫团队创作《文化里的中国》一书的初衷。

　　《文化里的中国》一书以铸牢中华民族共同体意识为主线，以弘扬中华优秀传统文化为主旋律，以构筑中华民族共有精神家园为主旨，以中华民族发展史为观照，立足于不同公众群体的阅读状况，以中英双语形式对"节气里的中国""诗词里的中国""节日里的中国"三个板块内容进行了有形、有感、有效的分析与阐释，并配备相关插图和视频作品二维码，以史鉴今、启迪未来，实现了"书中有视频，视频印书中"，是一本不断提升中华文化感召力、中国形象亲和力、中国话语说服力、国际舆论引导力的好读物，是张玫团队为北方民族大学举办 40 周年校庆和创建全国铸牢中华民族共同体意识教育示范校送上的一份贺礼。

　　五千年的历史文化和璀璨的中华文明是我们的自信之基、力量之源。二十四节气、诗词和节日是中国传统文化的重要组成部分，它们相互关联、相互交织，共同构成了中国丰富的文化景观以及中国人民的精神生活和文化传承，生动呈现了中华民族共同体的形成和发展历史，是立足于中国历史和中华民族发展史、讲好中国故事和中华民族故事的重要载体和素材。二十四节气是中国古代农业社会智慧的结晶，本书以读者喜闻乐见的方式讲述了与各个节气相关的习俗、农事活动和文化传承，体现了中国人对自然规律的深刻理解和尊重。诗词是中华文化宝库中的瑰宝，本书围绕诗人的情感、历史事件、社会风貌、写作风格等对经典古诗词进行了解读，为现代读者提供了一个了解古代中国、中华文明的窗口。传统节日是中华文化传承的重要载体，书中讲述了每个节日独特的起源、习俗和象征意义，有助于人们更好地理解中国的文化传统和民族精神。

　　《文化里的中国》以中英文对照、文图结合、扫码看视频等多种形式，传承和弘扬中华优秀传统文化，激发读者对中华文化的兴趣和热爱，加深读者对中国和中华文明突出特性的了解，引发读者对传统文化成为新时代中国人文化自信的精神力量的强烈共鸣。这部力作，是北方民族大学教师团队发挥专业优势和特色，服务"道中华"民族外宣工作品牌，"用英语传播中国声音、讲好中国故事和中华民族故事"，传承中华历史文脉，促进文化与文明交流互鉴的重要成果，也是让世界真正读懂中国、读懂中国人民、读懂中华民族以及更好地了解和关注中华文化的瑰宝，推动构建人类命运共同体的鲜活实践。

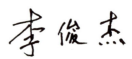

北方民族大学党委书记、校长

目 录

节气里的中国

Chinese Solar Terms

导 语
Introduction

在科技发达的当下，气象卫星、气象雷达、降雨量监测系统等可以帮助人们更好地进行农业生产活动。中国是农耕文化最悠久的国家之一，古代先民靠着自身对自然规律的把握和智慧总结出了一套农耕经验，这就是节气的雏形。二十四节气是指二十四时节和气候，是中国人归纳总结的一种用来指导农事和日常生活的时间知识体系，是中国传统历法的重要组成部分，是中国劳动人民长期经验的积累和智慧的结晶。

In the presence of technological advancement, meteorological satellites, weather radars and rainfall monitoring system can help people with agricultural activities better. China is one of the countries with the oldest agricultural cultures, and the ancient Chinese ancestors, relying on their understanding of nature and wisdom, formed a set of agricultural practices, which was the prototype of the 24 (Twenty-Four) solar terms. 24 solar terms refer to the 24 seasonal changes and climate patterns. This is a temporal knowledge system summarized and systematized by ancient Chinese people to guide agricultural activities and daily life. It is an essential component of China's calendar system, and it embodies the accumulated experience and wisdom of Chinese working people over a long period of time.

二十四节气作为中国古代先民认识世界的时间知识体系，已有数千年的历史。它起源于中国古代先民对太阳运行路径的观察和研究。根据太阳在黄道上的位置，中国古代先民将全年划分为二十四个时段，以节气的开始一日为节名。这种划分方法是古人基于对自然环境变化的观察和总结，根据自然季节循环的节律，以物候、气象、天文等自然现象为标志计划农耕周期、安排农耕劳作所创立的时间制度，是在阴阳历的基础上对全年的寒暑、雨露、霜雪等气候变化进一步细化与区分的时间秩序，是对大自然规律的反映。

As a knowledge system through which ancient Chinese understood the world, the 24 solar terms have a history spanning thousands of years. It originated from the observation and research of the sun's moving path by ancient Chinese ancestors. Based on the position of the sun on the ecliptic, the whole year is divided into 24 segments, with each named after the beginning of the solar term. This method of division was based on the observation and conclusion of changes in the natural environment by ancient people. According to the rhythm of natural seasonal cycles, with phenology, meteorology, astronomy, and other natural phenomena to plan the agricultural cycle, it is also a time system to arrange farming work. Based on the lunar and solar calendars, it further specifies and classifies the cold and heat, rain and dew, frost and snow, etc., reflecting the laws of nature.

二十四节气的形成经历了从两至、两分到四时八节，再到二十四个节气逐步完善的过程。根据《尚书·尧典》《周礼·春官宗伯》的记载，至迟在春秋时期，我们的先人就已经测定了春分、秋分、冬至、夏至这四个节气，即"四时"已经存在。战国末期，随着圭表测日技术的提高，先人逐渐确定了立春、立夏、立秋和立冬，它们与"四时"合称"八节"。随着物候的进一步丰富，二十四节气在秦汉时期则完全确立下来，《淮南子·天文训》中记述的二十四节气名称和顺序延续至今。汉武帝太初元年（公元前104年），邓平等制定的《太初历》颁行全国，二十四节气开始纳入国家历法，对后世产生了深远影响。

The formation of the 24 solar terms underwent a process from the simple division of two solstices and two equinoxes, to the four seasons and eight solar terms, and then gradually evolved into the 24 solar terms. According to records in *The Book of History* (*Shang Shu*) and *The Book of Rites* (*Zhou Li*), our ancestors had determined the four solar terms of Spring Equinox, Autumn Equinox, Winter Solstice, and Summer Solstice in the Spring and Autumn Period at the latest, which means the existence of the division of "four seasons". In the late Warring States Period, with the improvement of the gnomon's (a type of astronomical instrument) ability to measure the sun's shadow, the solar terms of "Start of Spring" "Start of Summer" "Start of Autumn" and "Start of Winter" were basically confirmed, collectively known as the "Eight Solar Terms" with the "four seasons". With the further enrichment of phenological indicators, the 24 solar terms were fully established in the Qin and Han dynasties. The names and sequence of the 24 solar terms described in the *Huai Nan Zi* have been passed down to the present day. In first year of Taichu during the reign of Emperor Wu of Han (104 BCE), the Taichu calendar formulated by Deng Ping and others was issued nationwide, incorporating the 24 solar terms into the national calendar. This exerted a profound influence on later generations.

二十四节气分为立春、雨水、惊蛰、春分、清明、谷雨、立夏、小满、芒种、夏至、小暑、大暑、立秋、处暑、白露、秋分、寒露、霜降、立冬、小雪、大雪、冬至、小寒、大寒。通过观察太阳在黄道上的位置来确定，每个节气持续的时间大概为十五天。

The 24 solar terms are: Start of Spring, Rain Water, Awakening of Insects, Spring Equinox, Pure Brightness, Grain Rain, Start of Summer, Grain Buds, Grain in Ear, Summer Solstice, Minor Heat, Major Heat, Start of Autumn, End of Heat, White Dew, Autumn Equinox, Cold Dew, Frost's Descent, Start of Winter, Minor Snow, Major Snow, Winter Solstice, Minor Cold and Major Cold. According to the position of the sun on the ecliptic, each solar term lasts about 15 days.

春季有立春到谷雨六个节气。立春意味着春天的开始，是气温回升、准备农耕的时节；雨水时节降雨增多、雨量渐大；惊蛰时节"春雷响，万物长"；春分前后万物复苏、生机勃勃；清明时节大地呈现春和景明之象，既是扫墓祭祖的肃穆节日，也适合郊外踏青游玩；谷雨时节降水量再次增加，气温迅速升高。

Spring includes six solar terms from Start of Spring to Grain Rain. Start of Spring marks the beginning of spring, and symbolizes the start of warmer temperatures and the preparation for farming. Rain Water signifies the increase in precipitation. During the Awakening of Insects, spring thunderstorms occur, and all things come to life. Around Spring Equinox, everything revives, and vitality flourishes. Pure Brightness presents a clear and bright scene, serving as a solemn occasion for tomb-sweeping and ancestor worship, as well as a festival for outdoor excursions. Finally, during Grain Rain, precipitation increases again, and temperatures rise rapidly.

夏季有立夏到大暑六个节气。立夏是夏季的第一个节气，标示着万物进入生长旺季；小满时节南方雨水充盈，北方小麦满而不盈、满而不溢；芒种时节南方种稻，北方收麦；夏至是一年中白昼最长、黑夜最短的一天；小暑、大暑时节天气炎热，雷暴频繁。

Summer includes six solar terms from Start of Summer to Major Heat. Start of Summer is the first term of summer, indicating the peak season for the growth of all things. During Grain Buds, southern regions experience abundant rainfall, while northern wheat is full but not overflowing. Grain in Ear is time for rice planting in the south and wheat harvesting in the north. Summer Solstice is the day with the longest daylight and the shortest night of the year in the northern hemisphere. As the weather is hot during Minor Heat and Major Heat, thunderstorms become frequent.

秋季有立秋到霜降六个节气。立秋是秋季的开始，万物从繁茂生长趋向成熟；处暑意味着炎热酷暑即将过去；白露时节天气逐渐由闷热转向凉爽，寒生露凝；秋分这天昼夜相等，此后温差逐渐加大；寒露以后，气温不断下降；霜降是秋季的最后一个节气，天气变冷，标志着即将告别秋季，迎来冬季。

Autumn includes six solar terms from Start of Autumn to Frost's Descent. Start of Autumn marks the beginning of autumn, as all things transit from lush growth to maturity. End of Heat signifies the end of scorching summer heat. During White Dew, the weather gradually changes from stuffiness to coolness, becoming colder and dewier. Autumn Equinox brings about equal day and night, with temperature differences gradually increasing since that day. Following Cold Dew, temperatures continue to drop, and Frost's Descent marks the final solar term of autumn, signaling the onset of colder weather and the impending arrival of winter.

冬季有立冬到大寒六个节气。立冬是冬季的开始，意味着万物进入休养生息状态；小雪、大雪时节气温显著下降，天气寒冷；冬至是一年中白昼最短、黑夜最长的一天；小寒和大寒是我国大部分地区最冷的时期，俗语说"小寒大寒，冷成冰团"。

Winter includes six solar terms from Start of Winter to Major Cold. Start of Winter marks the beginning of winter, symbolizing the entry of all things into a state of rest and recuperation. During Minor Snow and Major Snow, temperatures noticeably drop, bringing cold weather. Winter Solstice is the day with the shortest day and the longest night in a year in the northern hemisphere. Minor Cold and Major Cold represent the coldest periods in most regions of China, with a common saying that goes, "Minor Cold, Major Cold, cold as ice."

二十四节气在农事活动中发挥了重要作用，农民可以根据气候和季节的变化，精确地安排农作物的种植、管理和收获，提高农业生产的效率和质量。随着中华文化几千年的发展，二十四节气也被补充和丰富了更多有用且有效的内涵，超越了原本的农耕经验和实践，而深入人们的生活中。例如，惊蛰是春季养生的关键时期，人们可以根据惊蛰节气的到来，调整饮食和生活习惯，增强身体的抵抗力；立秋要"贴秋膘"，寒露和霜降则是秋季养生的重点时期；冬至日昼夜长短变化明显，人们可以在冬至节气到来之时，调整作息时间和饮食习惯，保持身体健康。

The 24 solar terms play an important role in agricultural activities. Farmers can precisely plan the planting, management, and harvesting of crops based on the changes in climate and seasons, thereby enhancing the efficiency and quality of agricultural production. With the development of Chinese culture over thousands of years, the 24 solar terms have been enriched with more useful and effective contents, extending beyond the original agricultural wisdom and practice to become an integral part of people's lives. For example, Awakening of

Insects is a critical period for health care in spring. People can adjust their diet and lifestyle to enhance their resistance to illnesses with the approach of Awakening of Insects. People eat meat during Start of Autumn, and Cold Dew and Frost's Descent are important periods for autumn health preservation. Winter Solstice sees noticeable changes in the length of day and night, and prompts people to adjust their daily routines and diets to keep healthy.

中国人独创的二十四节气，在国际气象界被誉为"中国第五大发明"。它不仅是黄河流域农业地区的时序指南，也是中国多民族、多地区的时间坐标；不仅是中国人自然哲学观念的生动体现，也是海外华人与祖国历史文化发生联系并加强文化认同的文化遗产。2016 年 11 月 30 日，联合国教科文组织保护非物质文化遗产政府间委员会评审通过了中国申报的"二十四节气——中国人通过观察太阳周年运动而形成的时间知识体系及其实践"非物质文化遗产项目，"二十四节气"被正式列入联合国教科文组织人类非物质文化遗产代表作名录。

The 24 solar terms, created independently by the Chinese people, are acclaimed as "the fifth great invention of China" in the international meteorological community. They not only serve as a seasonal guide for agriculture in the Yellow River area but also function as temporal coordinates for various ethnic groups and regions in China. They vividly reflect the Chinese people's philosophical concepts about nature and serve as a cultural heritage that reinforces the connection between overseas Chinese with their homeland's history and culture, strengthening cultural identity. On November 30, 2016, the Intergovernmental Committee for the Safeguarding of the Intangible Cultural Heritage of UNESCO approved the application submitted by China for the project "Twenty-Four Solar Terms: the time knowledge system and its practice formed by Chinese people through observing the annual movement of the sun". The Twenty-Four Solar Terms was officially inscribed in the UNESCO Representative List of the Intangible Cultural Heritage of Humanity.

你知道我国古代有哪些与二十四节气相关的礼仪吗？你知道哪些与二十四节气相关的有趣的物候知识和英语表达呢？下面请欣赏"节气里的中国"系列作品和精彩视频！

Do you know about the ceremonial rituals associated with the 24 solar terms in ancient times? Are you aware of the interesting phenological knowledge and English expressions related to the 24 solar terms? Please enjoy our "Chinese Solar Terms" series and exciting videos!

立　春
Start of Spring

扫码看视频

　　所谓"一年之计在于春"，立春自古以来就是一个重大节日。"立"是"开始"的意思；"春"既是温暖，鸟语花香，也是生长，耕耘播种。自秦代以来，中国就一直以立春作为春季的开始。在立春之日迎春已有很长历史。

As an old saying goes, "A year's plan starts with spring." Start of Spring has been an important festival since ancient times. "Li" means "beginning", and "Spring" suggests warmth, with birds' tweets and fragrance of flower. Spring is also a time for growth, when cultivation and sowing take place. Since the Qin Dynasty, Start of Spring has been taken as the beginning of spring in China. The custom of welcoming the spring on this day has a long history.

立春在每年公历的 2 月 3、4 或 5 日交节，是农历二十四节气中的第一个节气。在人们的心中，春意味着万物生长、农家播种。春天伊始，让我们一起走近立春，了解立春吧。

Start of Spring, starting annually on one day from February 3rd to 5th in the solar calendar, is the first of the 24 solar terms in the lunar calendar. In the hearts of people, spring signifies the growth of all things and the time for farmers to sow seeds. As the season of spring begins, let us approach Start of Spring and learn more about it.

农家岁首又谋耕
Planning for Agricultural Production in the Beginning of Year

立春后，寒消暖长，气温回升，又到了一年春耕春播时。俗话说："立春一年端，种地早盘算。"立春过后，备好种子和其他春耕生产物资，只待气温回暖，便可开展当年的春耕春播生产工作。

After Start of Spring, the coldness dissipates and the warmth grows; the temperature rises. It's time for spring ploughing and sowing again. As the saying goes, "Start of Spring is the beginning of a year; we should make early plans for planting." After Start of Spring, farmers prepare seeds and other spring ploughing production material. When the temperature is high enough, they will soon carry out the spring ploughing and sowing.

养生之道
Health Preservation Instructions

立春养生主要是护肝。人们应顺应自然界的规律，早睡早起，保持心情愉悦。由于立春之后的一段时间往往冷暖不定，因此要当心"倒春寒"的侵扰。要想杀菌并防寒，饮食方面可多吃大蒜、洋葱、芹菜等食物。另外，立春之后喝花茶有助于驱散冬季聚集在人体内的寒气和邪气。

In terms of health care, the focus is primarily on protecting the liver. People should also follow the natural laws, going to bed early and rising early. Keep a cheerful mood. For a period of time after Start of Spring, the temperature is still variable. Beware of the invasion of the "late spring cold". To sterilize and prevent cold, people can eat more garlics, onions, celeries and other foods. In addition, drinking scented tea can help dispel the cold and evil factors accumulated in the human body in winter after Start of Spring.

 游春
Spring Outing

立春时节，很多地区都有游春的习俗。人们纷纷装扮起来，集体游春。先是报春人打扮成公鸡的样子走在队伍最前面，之后一群人抬着桑木和泥土等材料做成的春牛，后面的人有打扮成牧童牵牛的，有打扮成大头娃娃送春桃的，还有打扮成燕子的……游春就是可以开始踏青的信号，从立春到端午之前都是踏青的好时候。

There is a custom of spring outing in many regions during Start of Spring. People will also dress up for their own parades. A harbinger of spring, dressed up as a rooster, would walk at the forefront of the team, followed by a group of people carrying a spring cattle made of mulberry woods and mud. Others in the parade dress in various costumes, such as herdsmen leading oxen, characters with oversized heads distributing spring peaches, and performers dressed as swallows... Spring outing is the signal for taking a spring outing. The period from Start of Spring until the Dragon Boat Festival is considered an excellent time for taking a walk in the countryside.

 结尾
Ending

春天是美好的，也是短暂的。立春亦如立人生，美好的时光易逝，我们怎能不倍加珍惜？

Spring is beautiful yet fleeting. The onset of spring is akin to the establishment of life. As beautiful moments elapse swiftly, how can we not cherish them even more?

 雨 水
Rain Water

扫码看视频

雨水是二十四节气中的第二个节气。雨水节气一般在公历 2 月 18、19 或 20 日交节。时至雨水节气，太阳的直射点由南半球逐渐向赤道靠近。这时的北半球，日照时间和强度都在增加，气温回升较快，来自海洋的暖湿空气开始活跃，并渐渐向北挺

雨水

进。与此同时，冷空气在减弱的趋势中不甘示弱，与暖空气频繁地交锋，形成降雨。雨水节气的含义是降雨开始。俗话说"春雨贵如油"，适宜的降水对农作物的生长很重要。

Rain Water is the second solar term of the 24 solar terms. It normally starts from February 18th, 19th or 20th in the solar calendar. During Rain Water, the point of direct sunlight gradually approaches the equator from the southern hemisphere. And in the northern hemisphere, sunshine duration and intensity are increasing and strengthening, and the temperature is increasing quickly. The warm and moist air from the ocean becomes active and gradually moves to the north. At the same time, the cold air, though in the weakening trend, collides with the warm air frequently and results in precipitation. Rain Water means the beginning of rainfall. Just as the saying goes, "The spring rainfall is as precious as oil." Proper precipitation is crucial for the growth of crops.

天气
Weather Conditions

雨水时节，天气变化不定，是全年寒潮出现最多的时节之一，乍暖还寒的天气会对农作物的生长及人们的健康带来危害。关于雨水的谚语中，有根据冷暖来预测后期天气的，如"冷雨水，暖惊蛰""暖雨水，冷惊蛰"；还有根据风的情况来预测后期天气的，如"雨水东风起，伏天必有雨"等。

The weather is unpredictable during Rain Water, when cold waves occur most frequently across the whole year. The climate which varies from hot to cold impacts the growth of crops and human health. Some referred to the temperature during Rain Water to forecast future weather, hence the sayings "Cold Rain Water suggests warm Awakening of Insects" and "Warm Rain Water suggests cold Awakening of Insects". Additionally, there are predictions about future weather based on the wind, such as "If the east wind rises on Rain Water, there will surely be rain during the hottest days of the year."

气候
Climate

在黄河流域，雨水之前天气寒冷，时有下雪；雨水之后雪渐少而雨渐多。在淮河以南地区，雨水后雨水较多，应做好农田清沟沥水和中耕除草工作。

In the Yellow River basin, it's cold before Rain Water and sometimes snows; after Rain Water, the snow is light and the rain is heavy. In the southern part of the Huaihe River, there is more rainfall after Rain Water, making ditches cleaning and water draining, cultivation and weeding in farmland a necessity.

农事活动
Farming Activities

雨水前后，油菜、冬麦普遍返青生长，对水分的要求较高，这时适宜的降水对作物的生长特别重要。

During the period around Rain Water, rapeseed and winter wheat generally turn from yellow to green and begin to grow again, requiring a higher amount of moisture. At this time, appropriate precipitation is particularly important for the growth of crops.

结尾
Ending

雨水至，万物萌动，是春天要来了，让我们一起去拥抱春天吧！

When Rain Water falls, everything becomes active. Spring is coming, and let's embrace it together!

惊 蛰
Awakening of Insects

扫码看视频

惊蛰是二十四节气中的第三个节气，也是仲春时节的开始，在每年公历 3 月 5、6 或 7 日交节，这时太阳正好运行至黄经 345°。在二十四节气之中，惊蛰反映的是生物受节律变化影响而出现萌发生长的现象。

Awakening of Insects is the third solar term, and also marks the beginning of the mid-spring season. The sun reaches at an ecliptic longitude of 345° on one day from March 5th to 7th every year in the solar calendar. Among all the 24 solar terms, Awakening of Insects reflects the germination and growth of all creatures affected by biorhythm changes.

春耕时节
Spring Farming Season

这个节气处于春季，是春耕的繁忙时期。又因这个节气雨水增加，有利于作物的种植，所以大家纷纷忙碌起来。江南小麦已经拔节，油菜已经开花，果树也纷纷被种下……

Falling on spring, Awakening of Insects is also a busy period of spring farming. Due to the increased rainfall during this solar term, which is beneficial for crop planting, everyone gets busy. The wheat in the south of the Yangtze River is at the elongation stage. The rapeseed is in bloom, and fruit trees are being planted in the fields...

惊蛰吃梨
Eating Pears in Awakening of Insects

惊蛰时节万物复苏，需要注意防寒保暖。此外，气候比较干燥，很容易使人口干舌燥、外感咳嗽。所以，民间素有"惊蛰吃梨"的习俗，梨可以生食，也可蒸、榨汁、烤或者煮水后食用。吃梨助益脾气，令五脏和平。此时，饮食起居应顺肝之性，以增强体质，抵御病菌的侵袭。

Awakening of Insects is a time when everything comes back to life. It's crucial to keep warm during Awakening of Insects. As the climate is relatively dry, people tend to feel dry in their mouths and parched in their throats, and have a cough. Therefore, there is a folk custom of eating pears during Awakening of Insects. Pears can be eaten raw, steamed, juiced, roasted or boiled in water. Eating pears is beneficial for the spleen, helping to reconcile the internal

惊蛰

organs. At this time, one's diet and lifestyle should conform to the nature of the liver so as to strengthen the physique against the invasion of pathogens.

"打小人" 驱赶霉运
"Beating Villains" to Ward off Bad Luck

惊蛰预示着农历二月份的开始。雷声会唤醒所有蛰伏的蛇、虫，所以，古时惊蛰当日，人们会手持艾草，熏家中四角，以香味驱赶蛇、虫、鼠，驱散霉味。久而久之，该习俗渐渐演变成不顺心者拍打对头人、驱赶霉运的习俗，亦即"打小人"的前身。

The arrival of Awakening of Insects marks the beginning of February in the lunar calender. All snakes and insects that are in hibernation will be woken up by the sound of thunder. On that day in ancient times, people would hold wormwood to smoke every corner of the house, driving away snakes, insects, rats and moldy smells with the scent. Over time, this practice gradually evolved into a custom for those experiencing misfortune to beat their opponents and expel bad luck, and later developed into the custom of "beating villains".

结尾
Ending

与冬惜别，与春相拥。冬去春来又一年，珍惜当下是关键。

As we bid farewell to winter, we embrace spring. Another brand-new year is around the corner, and it is crucial to cherish the present.

春 分
Spring Equinox

扫码看视频

春分，是春天的第四个节气。春分这一天，白天黑夜平分，各十二个小时。春分，一般在每年公历 3 月 20 或 21 日交节，正好处在春季三个月的当中，平分春季，故为春分。

Spring Equinox is the fourth solar term of spring. On the day of Spring Equinox, the day and night are divided equally, each having 12 hours. Spring Equinox usually falls on March 20th or 21st in the solar calendar, making the midpoint of spring and dividing it equally, hence its name.

民俗传统
Folk Customs

春分这天，历来有春祭的传统，包括祠堂祭祖、扫墓等。还有"立春蛋"，这项中国传统起源于四千年前，当时是为了庆祝春天的到来。人们还会在这一天画春牛图，寓意春耕顺利。

On the day of Spring Equinox, there is a tradition called spring offerings, which see people worship ancestors at ancestral temples and sweep tombs on this day. The tradition of "Erecting Eggs" originated 4,000 years ago to celebrate the arrival of spring. People also

draw pictures of spring cattle on this day, in the hope of the smooth spring ploughing in the year.

农事活动
Farming Activities

一场春雨一场暖，春雨过后忙耕田。春分过后，越冬作物进入快速生长阶段，这时要加强田间管理。由于气温回升快，作物需水量相对较大，因此农民朋友要加强蓄水保墒。

It's gradually getting warmer after raining in spring and farmers get busy ploughing. After Spring Equinox, the overwintering crops enter the fast-growth stage, and field management should be strengthened. As the temperature rises quickly, the water demand is relatively large. Farmers should strengthen water storage and conservation.

生活提示
Life Tips

在春分时节，减衣不宜过早，还要多喝水、定时作息、规律睡眠。饮食上宜选清淡、甘温之品，忌酸涩。

At the time of Spring Equinox, we shouldn't take off the warm clothes too early, but drink more water, have regular work and rest. For the diet, it's suggested to consume food that is light in flavor, sweet and warm in nature, and avoid food that is sour and astringent.

结尾
Ending

春天意味着生机，希望你可以和朋友们沐浴着春光，一起奔赴美好的生活和未来。

Spring symbolizes vitality and hope. May you bask in the spring sunshine with friends and head towards a wonderful life and future together.

清 明
Pure Brightness

扫码看视频

　　清明，是春季里的第五个节气，在每年公历的 4 月 4、5 或 6 日交节。前有仲春繁花似锦，后有暮春绿树成荫，而清明位于其中，气清景明，万物生长于此时，皆清洁而明净，是为清明。

　　Pure Brightness is the fifth solar term in spring. It starts from April 4th, 5th or 6th every year in the solar calendar. Flowers bloom in February in lunar calendar, and the trees shade in March in lunar calender. Pure Brightness is right between the two periods. At this time, the weather is clear while the scenery is beautiful, and everything begins to grow, thus, it is called Pure Brightness.

民俗传统
Folk Customs

清明最显著的一个特点是，它不仅是一个节气，还是一个传统节日。清明又称扫墓节，这天历来有祭祖踏青的传统。

清明节更是中国传统的重大春祭节日，背后蕴含着中华民族的深厚凝聚力和认同感，把中国的自然风俗和人文气质融为一体，体现了古人历来所追求的"天、地、人"的和谐。

One of the most distinctive features of Pure Brightness is that it serves both as a solar term and a traditional festival.

As a festival, it can also be called Tomb-sweeping Day, when people would worship ancestors and take a spring outing. The day is a major festival in spring for the traditional rite for ancestor-worshiping, which reflects a deep cohesion and sense of identity of the Chinese nation. It is an integration of China's natural customs and humanistic temperament. It also embodies the pursuit of the harmony of "heaven, earth and human" since ancient times.

农事活动
Farming Activities

说起清明气候，大家可能会想到"清明时节雨纷纷"，其实这是我国大部分南方地区的写照。清明前后，南方的降雨增多，相比之下，北方则雨量不足，甚至有"春雨贵如油"的说法。

Speaking of the climate of Pure Brightness, people may think of the scene of "a drizzling rain falls like tears on the Mourning Day". In fact, this is primarily a portrayal of the southern China. Around Pure Brightness, the rainfall in the south increases, while that in the north is insufficient, and there is even a saying that "The rain in spring is as precious as oil".

生活提示
Life Tips

清明前后气温变化较大，一转暖，细菌病毒便极易滋生，请一定要勤洗手、常通风。对花粉过敏的朋友，出行时要注意防护。此时节可适时晚睡早起，多吃时令多汁蔬果，多饮水，以清肺润燥。

The temperatures change dramatically around Pure Brightness. Once it gets warmer, bacteria and viruses thrive easily. So, wash hands and ventilate frequently. If you are allergic to pollen, take precautions when going out. At this time, you can go to bed late and get up early appropriately, eat more seasonal juicy fruits and vegetables, drink more water so as to clear lungs and moisten dryness.

结尾
Ending

清明祭祀的目的不仅是缅怀祖先，还在于记住先人的奋斗历史，传承先人的奋斗精神。回望历史长河，让我们在生活中拥有一颗强大的心。

The purpose of sacrifice in Pure Brightness is not only to remember our ancestors and their struggle history, but also to inherit their spirits. Let's have a strong heart in life looking back on the long river of history.

谷 雨
Grain Rain

扫码看视频

"雨生百谷"即为谷雨，谷雨是春季的最后一个节气，于每年公历 4 月 19、20 或 21 日交节。此时降水明显增加，田中的秧苗初插、作物新种，非常需要雨水的滋润。谷雨与雨水、小满、小雪、大雪等节气一样，都是反映降水现象的节气，是古代农耕文化对于节令的反映。

"Rain gives birth to all grains", hence the name of Grain Rain. It is the last solar term of spring, and starts from April 19th, 20th or 21st every year in the solar calendar. During Grain Rain, the precipitation increases significantly, the seedlings in the field and new crops are in great need of rain. Grain Rain, like Rain Water, Grain Buds, Minor Snow, Major Snow and other solar terms, reflects the precipitation phenomena as well as the close connection between ancient farming culture and the season.

民俗传统
Folk Customs

古时有"走谷雨"的风俗。谷雨这天，人们走村串亲，或者到野外走一圈，寓意亲近自然，强身健体。

In ancient times, there was a custom of "Walking on Grain Rain". On this day, people would walk through the village to visit relatives, and some just take a walk around the field to stay close with the nature and keep fit.

南方有谷雨摘茶的习俗。传说喝了谷雨这天采的茶能清火、辟邪、明目等。所以，不管谷雨这天的天气如何，人们都会去茶山摘一些新茶回来喝。

The custom of picking tea in southern China: According to folklore, consuming tea picked on this day is believed to have various health benefits, such as clearing heat within the body, warding off evil spirits, and improving eyesight. Therefore, no matter what the weather is on Grain Rain, people will pick and brew some fresh tea.

北方有谷雨食香椿的习俗。谷雨前后是香椿上市的时节，这时的香椿醇香爽口、营养价值高，有"雨前香椿嫩如丝"之说。香椿具有提高机体免疫力、健胃、理气、止泻、抗菌等功效。

The custom of eating Chinese toon in northern China: The Chinese toon normally hits the market around Grain Rain because of its fragrance, refreshing taste and nutrition. There is a saying that "The Chinese toon before Grain Rain tastes as tender as silk". The Chinese toon has the effects of enhancing immunity, promoting digestion, regulating "qi", stopping diarrhea, killing bacteria, etc.

农事活动
Farming Activities

俗话说："谷雨时节种谷天，南坡北洼忙种棉。"谷雨是春季的最后一个节气。中国南方大部分地区这时雨水丰沛，每年第一场大雨一般出现在这段时间，对水稻栽插和玉米、棉花苗期生长有利。

As an old saying goes, "Grain Rain marks the season of grain planting, and cotton is planted on slopes in southern China and lowlands in northern China." Grain Rain is the last solar term of spring. There will be abundant rain in most parts of southern China, and the first heavy rain of the year usually occurs during this period, which is beneficial for rice transplanting and the growth of corn and cotton.

 生活提示
Life Tips

由于谷雨节气后降雨增多，空气中的湿度逐渐增加，所以谷雨节气后是神经痛的发作期。天气转暖，人们室外活动增加，但由于北方地区的桃花、杏花等开放，柳絮四处飞扬，因此过敏体质的人应注意预防花粉症及过敏性鼻炎、过敏性哮喘等。在饮食上应减少高蛋白质、高热量食物的摄入。

Due to the increase of rainfall after Grain Rain, the humidity in the air gradually rises. So Grain Rain is also a period of onset for neuralgia. As the weather warms up, outdoor activities have increased. Peach blossom and apricot flowers bloom in northern regions, and willow catkins fly everywhere. Therefore, those who are allergic to them should pay attention to the prevention of hay fever, allergic rhinitis and allergic asthma. In terms of diet, intake of high-protein and high-calorie foods should be reduced.

结尾
Ending

谷雨时节，万物茁壮成长，又是一个美好的时节。谷雨的故事在开始，春天的故事在萌芽。我们一起期待未来的收获。

During Grain Rain season, everything grows vigorously, marking another beautiful time. The story of Grain Rain begins, and the story of spring sprouts. We look forward to future harvest together.

立　夏
Start of Summer

扫码看视频

立夏是二十四节气的第七个节气，表示夏天的开始，在每年公历 5 月 5、6 或 7 日交节。立夏还是一个传统的岁时礼俗节日，周代在立夏这一天，天子要率三公九卿和众大夫，到城南郊外迎夏，并举行祭祀火神祝融的仪式。

Start of Summer is the 7th of the 24 solar terms, signifying the start of summer. It starts from May 5th, 6th or 7th in the solar calendar. Start of Summer is a traditional festival of customs. Back in the Zhou Dynasty, the emperor would lead senior officials and ministers to the southern outskirts of the capital to welcome the summer. A ceremony was also held to offer sacrifices to the God of Fire, Zhurong.

汉代也沿承此俗，《后汉书·祭祀志》载："立夏之日，迎夏于南郊，祭赤帝祝融，车旗服饰皆赤，歌《朱明》，八佾舞《云翘》之舞。"到宋代，礼仪更趋烦琐。至明代始有"尝新"风俗。

The Han Dynasty also inherited this custom. According to *The Book of the Eastern Han Dynasty*, on Start of Summer, the emperor and officials welcomed the summer at the southern outskirts of the capital and held a ceremony to worship the god of fire Zhurong. The clothing, flags, and vehicles were all in red. The song *Zhu Ming* was sung and the dance *Cloud Wing Dance* was also performed. In the Song Dynasty, the ceremony became more complex. It wasn't until the Ming Dynasty that the custom of "Eating fresh and seasonal food" began.

民俗传统
Folk Customs

清代《帝京岁时纪胜》载"立夏取平时曝晒之米粉春芽，并用糖面煎作各色果叠，相互馈送"，并用柳枝穿果叠做小儿食品。江浙一带还有立夏吃花饭（也称"吃补食"）的习俗。

According to *The Records of Seasonal Customs in the Capital during the Qing Dynasty*, during Start of Summer, people would take the sun-dried rice flour and spring sprouts and fry them into various treats using sugar, and exchange them with each other. Willow branches were also used to thread the treats for children. In Jiangsu and Zhejiang provinces, there is also a tradition of eating Huafan during Start of Summer, which is also called "Eating Supplement Food".

民间习俗还有"立夏吃蛋，石头都踩烂"的说法，说立夏时吃鸡蛋、鸭蛋可以增强体质，还可以耐暑。还有立夏食笋、立夏喝酒、立夏见"三新"（樱桃、青梅、麦子）等习俗，都是在立夏这天。南方地区旧时逢立夏日，各家蒸新茶，并配以各种水果，馈赠亲朋好友。

In folk customs, there is a saying, "Eat eggs on Start of Summer, and you can even tread on rocks until they break." It is believed that consuming eggs, whether chicken or duck eggs, during Start of Summer can enhance one's physical strength and increase resistance to the heat. Some people eat bamboo shoots, some drink alcohol, and some eat "Three New Things" (cherry, green plum, wheat) on Start of Summer. In the southern regions, it was customary to steam fresh tea on the day of Start of Summer, accompanied by various fruits, which were then gifted to relatives and friends.

小满
Grain Buds

扫码看视频

　　"小满天逐热，温风沐麦圆。"诗歌中提到的"小满"即二十四节气中的第八个节气，也是夏季的第二个节气，于每年公历 5 月 20、21 或 22 日交节。小满之名，有两层含义。第一，与降水有关。小满节气期间，南方的暴雨增多，降水频繁，民谚云"小满小满，江河渐满"。小满中的"满"，指雨水之盈。第二，与作物小麦有关。在北方地区，小满节气期间降雨较少，甚至无雨，这个"满"不是指降水，而是指麦粒的饱满程度。

　　"It's getting hotter as Grain Buds comes; wheat grains grow plump in the warm wind." Grain Buds mentioned in this poem is the eighth of the 24 solar terms, and the second solar term of summer. It starts from May 20th, 21st or 22nd every year in the solar calendar. The Chinese pinyin of Grain Buds, Xiaoman, has two meanings. First, it is related to precipitation. In the period of Grain Buds, heavy rainfall begins to increase and precipitation becomes frequent in southern China. As the saying goes, "A heavy rainfall during Grain Buds makes the river full." Second, it is related to agriculture, specifically, wheat. In the northern region, as there is little or no rainfall in the period of Grain Buds, so the "fullness" here has nothing to do with precipitation, but with the fullness of wheat.

民俗传统
Folk Customs

　　小满这天，不同地方的习俗也会不一样。在江浙一带的农村，养蚕极为盛行，而蚕宝宝很娇气以至于非常难养，因此江浙一带在小满时节会过祈蚕节，以祈求"天物"的宽恕和养蚕有个好收成。在关中地区，每年麦子快要成熟的时候，出嫁的女儿都要到娘家去探望，问候夏收的准备情况。这一风俗叫作"麦梢黄，女看娘"，极富诗意。

　　On this day, the customs differ in places. In rural areas of Jiangsu and Zhejiang, sericulture is prevalent, but the baby silkworms are quite delicate and difficult to raise. Therefore, the Silkworm Praying Festival is held in the period of Grain Buds to seek forgiveness from the "heavenly beings" and to pray for a bountiful harvest in silkworm rearing. In the Guanzhong region in central Shaanxi Province, when the wheat is about to ripen each year, married daughters would visit their natal homes to care for the preparations for the summer harvest. This custom, called "wheat into yellow, women back to moms", is quite poetic.

农事活动
Farming Activities

小满节气时正值初夏。蚕茧结成，正待采摘续丝。江南地区，自小满之日起，蚕妇煮蚕茧，开动纺丝车缫丝。人们还取菜籽至油车坊磨油，天旱则用水车引水入田。此时是农家最繁忙的季节，俗语说"小满动三车"，说的就是丝车、油车和水车。民间还会举行"抢水"仪式，由年长执事者召集各户，各户在确定好的日期的黎明时分燃起火把，在水车车基上吃麦糕、麦饼、麦团。执事者以敲锣为号，群人以击器相和，踏上事先装好的水车，数十辆一起踏动，把河水引灌入田，至河浜水光方止。在黄河中下游流域的一些省份，这时农民正忙着收麦打场；在珠江流域，农民则播种秋稻；在东北地区，这时正是棉花和大豆下种的时期，高粱刚刚长出，农民必须锄去杂草，剪除劣苗。

Grain Buds falls in early summer. Cocoons are formed, and the silk is ready to be picked. In the Jiangnan region, from the day of Grain Buds, silkworm women begin to boil cocoons and reel silk on the spinning wheels. People also bring rapeseed to the oil mill to produce oil. In times of drought, water wheels are used to irrigate the fields. It is the busiest season for farmers. As the saying goes, "Grain Buds gets three carts running." These "three carts" respectively refer to the machines for making silk, extracting oil and diverting water. There is also a "water grabbing" ceremony, in which the elderly supervisor gathers households, the households light torches at dawn on the fixed date, and they eat wheat cakes, wheat pies, and wheat balls on the base of the waterwheel. When the supervisor beats the gong, people will strike instruments to follow him. Then they will step on dozens of pre-installed waterwheels together to divert water from the river to the fields until the river is dried up. In some provinces in the middle and lower reaches of the Yellow River basin, farmers are busy threshing wheat. Autumn rice is sown in the Pearl River basin. In northeastern China, cotton and soybeans are planted, and the sorghum has just grown, so the weeds must be hoed and inferior seedlings cut.

小满

生活提示
Life Tips

　　小满时节南方高温多雨，在高温高湿交加的环境中，人体感觉湿热难耐，却又无法通过水分蒸发来保持热量的平衡。因此在阴雨或雾天里要少开窗户，避免湿气进入；在艳阳高照时，要多开窗通风；可利用空调的抽湿功能，保证室内空气湿度不高于60%。饮食上要多食用消热利湿的食物，如绿豆粥、荷叶粥、赤豆粥等，以方便将体内湿热之邪排出。

　　It is hot and rainy during Grain Buds in southern China. In the environment with high temperature and humidity, the human body cannot bear the discomfort and fails to maintain the balance of heat through water evaporation. In rainy or foggy days, keep windows open less to avoid moisture entering; when the sun is shining, open the window more frequently for ventilation; use the dehumidification function of the air conditioner to ensure that the indoor air humidity does not exceed 60%. Eat more foods that dissipate heat and moisture, such as mung bean porridge, lotus leaf porridge, red bean porridge, etc., to facilitate the expulsion of the internal dampness and heat.

结尾
Ending

　　小满小麦粒渐满，风吹草地绿色满，朝夕锻炼身体健。小满之日，希望大家：生活幸福要美满，学习虚心不自满，财源广进钱袋满，心胸坦荡少不满，完成工作要圆满，宏图大展志得意满。

When Grain Buds comes, the wheat is gradually full. The wind blows through the meadow and brings lush green. Our health comes easily only with everyday exercise. On Grain Buds, we wish you a happy and fulfilling life, with a humble learning attitude, high income, more open-mindedness and less dissatisfaction, as well as successful work and great ambitions that can be realized.

芒 种
Grain in Ear

扫码看视频

芒种是二十四节气的第九个节气、夏季的第三个节气，在每年公历 6 月 5、6 或 7 日交节。这个时节气温显著升高、雨量充沛、空气湿度大，适宜晚稻等谷类作物种植。芒种是古代农耕文化对于节令的反映。

Grain in Ear is the ninth of the 24 solar terms and the third one in summer. It starts from June 5th, 6th or 7th in the solar calendar, with rising temperature, abundant rainfall and high humidity, which is suitable for the planting of late rice and other cereal crops. Grain in Ear is a reflection of the ancient agrarian culture regarding the seasonal changes.

芒种节气在农耕上有着相当重要的意义。芒种节气适合种植谷类作物，是种植谷类作物的关键时间。对我国大部分地区来说，芒种之后将不再有最好的谷物种植时间。芒种还是一个忙碌的节气，这个时节，正是南方种稻与北方收麦之时。

Grain in Ear is of great significance in farming activities, during which it is proper to plant cereal crops. It is also a critical timing because after Grain in Ear, the best time to plant cereal crops will be gone in most parts of China. It is also a busy time for rice in southern China to be planted and wheat in northern China to be harvested.

民俗传统
Folk Customs

中国贵州东南部一带的侗族青年男女，在每年芒种前后都要打泥巴仗。当天，新婚夫妇由要好的男女青年陪同，集体插秧，边插秧边打闹，互扔泥巴。活动结束后，

检查战果，身上泥巴最多的人，就是最受欢迎的人。

Before and after the Grain in Ear, young men and women of the Dong ethnic group in southeastern Guizhou Province will hold a Mud Festival, when newlyweds will transplant rice seedlings with their best friends, while throwing mud at each other. In the end, the one with the most mud is definitely the most popular.

节气轶事
Anecdotes of Grain in Ear

根据作家刘心武在中国的一档揭秘《红楼梦》的节目中的讲述，芒种这一天被认为是贾宝玉的生日。与此同时，著名的黛玉葬花情节也发生在芒种这天。

According to the writer Liu Xinwu's statement about *A Dream in Red Mansions* in a Chinese TV program, it is believed that Jia Baoyu's birthday was on Grain in Ear. At the same time, the famous plot "Lin Daiyu's Elegy on Flowers" also took place on Grain in Ear.

结尾
Ending

芒种是一个忙碌的节气，我们要使自己的精神保持轻松、愉快的状态。夏日昼长夜短，午休可助消除疲劳，有利于健康。此外，我们还要注意多喝水哦！

Grain in Ear is a busy solar term. Keep relaxed and happy during Grain in Ear. In summer, when days are long and nights are short, taking a nap can help alleviate fatigue and promote health. And be sure to drink more water!

夏至
Summer Solstice

扫码看视频

"石鼎声中朝暮，纸窗影下寒温。"诗人范成大在《夏至》一诗中以此来描述夏至。夏至，是二十四节气中的第十个节气，于每年公历6月21或22日交节。以夏至日为起点，气温持续升高，一年中最热的时段将要到来，故有"夏至不过不热"的说法，而夏至也被人们称为一年中热暑即将到来的起始日，并因此得名。

"The morning and evening in the sound of the stone tripod, the cold and warm under the shadow of the paper window." This is how the poet Fan Chengda described Summer Solstice in his poem "Summer Solstice". Summer Solstice, the tenth solar term in the 24 solar terms, starts from June 21st or 22nd in the solar calendar. Taking Summer Solstice as the starting point, temperatures continue to rise, and the hottest period of the year is about to arrive. Hence, there is a saying, "It won't get hot until after Summer Solstice", and this day is also referred to by people as the beginning of the hot and sultry weather in the year, which is how it got its name.

民俗传统
Folk Customs

在夏至这一天，各地有着许多的民俗传统，如祭神祀祖、食夏至面、食夏至饼、夏至称人、互赠消夏之物等。民间常言"冬至饺子夏至面"，北京人在夏至这天讲究

吃凉面，以达到降火开胃的成效。南方的无锡人在夏至这天的早晨吃麦粥，中午吃馄饨，取混沌和合之意。有谚语说："夏至馄饨冬至团，四季安康人团圆。"吃过馄饨，便为孩童称体重，希望孩童成长得更健康。而在岭南一带，则有夏至吃荔枝的习俗。

On the day of Summer Solstice, there are numerous folk traditions around the country, such as offering sacrifices to ancestors, eating noodles of special spices, eating cakes of special ingredients, weighing people, and giving summer gifts to each other. As the folk saying goes, "(Chinese people prefer) dumplings on Winter Solstice and noodles on Summer Solstice". People in Beijing like eating cold noodles on Summer Solstice to relieve heat and promote appetite. In the south, people in Wuxi eat wheat porridge in the morning and wontons (馄饨, huntun) at noon, meaning the pursuit of harmony out of chaos (混沌 hundun, similar to the sound of 馄饨 huntun). There is a proverb that says, "With wontons on Summer Solstice and rice puddings on Winter Solstice, wish you health and reunion all the year around." After eating wontons, they will weigh their children, hoping that weight gain brings their kids health. In the Lingnan area, there is a custom of eating lychee on Summer Solstice.

农事活动
Farming Activities

民间有句俗话说"夏种不让晌"，意思是夏播工作要抓紧扫尾，已播的要加强管理，力争全苗，出苗后应及时定苗，移栽补缺。夏至时节，各种农田杂草和庄稼一样生长得很快，它们不仅与作物争水、争肥、争阳光，而且是多种病菌和害虫的寄主，因此农谚说"夏至不锄根边草，如同养下毒蛇咬"。夏至后也是雨水增多的季节，因此需要及时除草。

As the folk saying goes, "Summer farming is so busy that any noon should not be wasted." Summer sowing work should be finished soon around Summer Solstice. The sown crops need strengthened management to encourage sprouting. It's a timely need to fix the amount of seedlings in the field to ensure the healthy growth of the crops. The extra seedlings should be transplanted and those failing to sprout should be replaced with new ones. During Summer Solstice, various farmland weeds grow as fast as crops, not only competing for water, fertilizer and sunlight, but also hosting a variety of bacteria and pests. Therefore, farmers always say, "Keep weeds growing on Summer Solstice, like keeping a snake biting." After Summer Solstice, it comes the season of increased rain. Therefore, timely weeding is needed.

生活提示
Life Tips

　　夏至有雨三伏热，重阳无雨一冬晴。夏至后往往有高温天气袭来，阳气盛于外。夏至过后，阳极阴生，阴气居于内，所以饮食上要以清泄暑热、增进食欲为目的，多吃苦味食物，宜清补，忌夜食生冷、忌空腹饮茶、忌冷水洗浴、忌夜卧贪凉。

　　Proverb has it that "Rain on Summer Solstice suggests a hot summer, while no rain on the Double Ninth Festival suggests a sunny winter". After Summer Solstice usually comes the summer heat. It's a time when the Yang energy is prevailing, but after that, the Yin will go up and reside inside the body. After Summer Solstice, diet should be aimed at clearing heat and improving appetite. Light diet and bitter food are preferred. Some practices, such as eating cold food at night, drinking tea on an empty stomach, taking a cold bath and sleeping by cold wind all night, should be avoided.

结尾
Ending

夏至节气到，木槿花盛开，带来的是希望、幸运、幸福。夏至节气，提醒大家要注意养生保健、祛暑益气，愿清风徐来时你我皆可得福闲静，忘忧于心。

When Summer Solstice approaches, hibiscus is in full bloom, bringing us hope, luck and happiness. We should pay attention to health care, dispel the heat and nourish the "qi". May all of us be cheerful and trouble-free in tranquility when the breeze gently embraces us.

小 暑
Minor Heat

扫码看视频

绿树浓荫，时至小暑。小暑在每年公历 7 月 6、7 或 8 日交节。小暑是二十四节气之第十一个节气，也是夏季的第五个节气。小暑意味着天气热了起来，但并不是最热的时候。小暑之后，人们将一个接一个地迎来三个阶段的酷暑，中国人称之为"三伏"，意思是在这种天气人们不宜剧烈活动。小暑后一段时间就是"初伏"。

When the trees become lush, there comes Minor Heat. Minor Heat starts from 6th, 7th or 8th every year in the solar calendar. It is the 11th solar term of the 24 solar terms, and the fifth solar term of summer. Minor Heat means it is hot, but not the hottest. After Minor Heat, three phases of intense heat come one after another. The Chinese call it "Sanfu", which means that people should not engage in strenuous activities in such weather. After a period of Minor Heat is the "beginning of Fu".

民俗传统
Folk Customs

过去在中国南方地区民间有小暑"食新"习俗，即在小暑过后尝新米。农民将新割的稻谷碾成米后，做好饭供祀五谷大神和祖先，然后人人品尝新酒等。在北方地区有头伏吃饺子的传统，因为伏天人们往往食欲不振，而饺子在传统习俗里正是开胃解

馋的食物，且饺子的外形像元宝，吃饺子象征着福气满满。

In the past, there was a folk custom of "eating something new" during Minor Heat in southern China, that is, eating new rice after Minor Heat. Farmers would grind the newly-cut rice into rice grains and make a meal as a sacrifice to the God of the Five Grains and their ancestors, and then everyone would drink new wine and so on. In northern China, there is a tradition of eating dumplings on the first of the three 10-day periods (Sanfu Days, or Dogs Days) of the hot season. That is because people usually lose their appetites in Dog Days. In traditional customs, dumplings are the food for appetizer, and they are shaped like Yuanbao, ancient Chinese gold or silver ingots, so eating dumplings symbolizes "full of fortune".

在农历六月初六这一天，家家户户多会不约而同选择"晒伏"，就是把存放在箱柜里的衣服晾到外面接受阳光的曝晒，以去潮去湿、防霉防蛀。

A tradition called "Shai Fu" falls on June 6th of the lunar calendar. Every household would hang out the clothes stored in the wardrobe for sun exposure, to disperse moisture and prevent mildew.

小暑养生
Health Care during Minor Heat

小暑是人体阳气最旺盛的时候。中医认为，"春夏养阳"，所以人们要注意劳逸结合，保护体内的阳气。天气热的时候要喝汤或粥，用荷叶、土茯苓、扁豆、薏米、猪苓、

泽泻、木棉等材料煲成的消暑汤或粥，或甜或咸，非常适合在此节气食用。多吃水果也有益于防暑，但是不要食用过量，以免增加肠胃负担，严重时会造成腹泻。

Minor Heat is the most vigorous period of Yang energy in the human body. "Nourishing Yang in spring and summer" is a widely believed principle in traditional Chinese medicine, so people are supposed to strike a balance to preserve the Yang energy. When it is hot, it's a good choice to eat porridge. The soup or congee made of lotus leaves, poria cocos, lentils, pearl barley, grifola, alisma, kapok and other materials, sweet or salty, is very ideal during this solar term. Eating more fruits is also beneficial for heat prevention, but it doesn't mean you should overindulge. Having too much will increase the burden on the stomach and severe cases can come with diarrhea.

结尾
Ending

"倏忽温风至，因循小暑来。"小暑至，盛夏始。

"Breezes suddenly get warm, there comes Minor Heat." The arrival of Minor Heat marks the beginning of the midsummer.

大　暑
Major Heat

扫码看视频

大暑是夏季最后一个节气，在每年公历 7 月 22、23 或 24 日交节。夏天用尽全力掀起最后一波热浪，植物都被晒得冒出了"汗珠"，它们的根系在土壤中疯狂吸水。蒸腾作用是植物在烈日底下最快速的降温方式，因此植物在烈日高温下才能不被晒蔫或干枯。所以夏天爱出汗的你也要多喝水，否则也会"蔫"的。

Major Heat is the last solar term of summer, which starts from July 22nd, 23rd or 24th in the solar calendar. The last heat wave of summer is set off with all its strength, plants soaked in sweat and their roots absorbing water crazily in the soil. Transpiration is the fastest way for plants to cool down under the scorching sun and protect themselves from wilting or

drying up. If you sweat a lot in summer, you should drink more water, otherwise you will "wilt" too.

大暑三候："一候腐草为萤，二候土润溽暑，三候大雨时行。"每到大暑时节，由于气温偏高又有雨水，细菌容易滋生，许多枯死的植物潮湿腐化，到了夜晚，经常可以看到萤火虫在腐草败叶上飞来飞去寻找食物。另外，土壤高温潮湿，很适宜水稻等喜水作物的生长。在这雨热同季的潮热天气，随时都会有雨水落下。

There are three periods of Major Heat: First, rotten grass breeds fireflies; second, the soil moistens the humid summer; third, the rain pours frequently. Due to the high temperature and rainfall, bacteria are bred easily, and many dead plants turn moist and decay in this period. At night, fireflies can often be seen flying around on the rotten grass and seeking food. In addition, the soil is hot and humid, which is very suitable for the growth of water-loving crops such as rice. In this hot and humid season, rain may come at any time.

民俗传统
Folk Customs

大暑是三伏天的中伏。自古以来，民间有三伏天饮伏茶的习俗。顾名思义，伏茶是指三伏天饮的茶，这种由金银花、夏枯草、甘草等十多味草药煮成的茶水有清凉祛暑的作用。古时候，很多地方的农村都有个习俗，就是村里人会在村口的凉亭里放些茶水，免费给来往路人喝。每个凉亭里都有专人全天煮茶，保证供应。

Major Heat is in the middle of Sanfu Days. Since ancient times, there has been a folk custom of drinking herbal tea (Fu Tea) on the Sanfu Days. Fu Tea, as the name suggests, is a kind of tea for Sanfu Days. This kind of tea, which is made up of more than ten herbs such as honeysuckle, prunella vulgaris and liquorice, has the effect of cooling and relieving heat. Also, there was a custom in many rural areas that villagers would put some tea in the pavilion at the entrance of the village and give it to passers-by for free in ancient times. There were specially-assigned people in each pavilion who boiled tea all day long to ensure tea supply.

此外，晒伏姜也是大暑时重要的习俗。伏姜源自中国山西、河南等地，三伏天时人们会把生姜切片或者榨汁后与红糖搅拌在一起，装入容器中蒙上纱布，放于太阳下晾晒，待其充分融合后方可食用，伏姜对老寒胃、伤风咳嗽等有奇效。这也是"冬病夏治"的方式之一。吃了寒凉之物、受了雨淋或在空调房间里久待后，喝杯伏姜汤能及时消除肌体寒重造成的各种不适。

In addition, drying ginger is also an important activity on Major Heat. Fu Ginger (Ginger for Sanfu Days) originates from Shanxi, Henan and other places in China. On the Dog Days, people will mix ginger slices or juice with brown sugar, put them in containers, cover them with gauze, dry them in the sun and wait for the ingredients to integrate, and eat or drink them. The dried ginger has a marvelous effect on chronic cold stomach, cold cough and so on. This is also one of the ways to "treat winter diseases in summer". After you eat something cold, get caught in the rain or stay in an air-conditioned room for a long time, you can drink a cup of Fujiang soup. It will timely eliminate all kinds of discomfort caused by coldness in your body.

立 秋
Start of Autumn

扫码看视频

立秋，是二十四节气的第十三个节气，标志着秋季的起始。立秋在每年公历的8月7、8或9日交节。"立"，是开始之意；"秋"，意为禾谷成熟。整个自然界的变化是循序渐进的过程，立秋是阳气渐收、阴气渐长，由阳盛逐渐转变为阴盛的转折。在自然界，万物开始从繁茂成长趋向成熟。

Start of Autumn, the 13th solar term of the 24 solar terms, also marks the beginning of autumn. It starts from August 7th, 8th or 9th in the solar calendar. "Li" means the beginning, while "Autumn" means that the grain is ripe. The change of the whole nature is a gradual process. Start of Autumn is the time when Yang energy gradually recedes, whereas Yin energy gradually grows. It is a turning point of changing from Yang predominance to Yin predominance. During this time, things start to ripen from lush growth.

民俗传统
Folk Customs

立秋时，民间有祭祀土地神、庆祝丰收的习俗。在古代，在立秋收成之后，人们会挑选一个黄道吉日，一方面祭拜上苍，感谢祖先的庇佑；另一方面品尝新收获的米谷，以庆祝辛勤换来的收获。此外，民间还有在立秋这天"贴秋膘"（如吃肉）、"咬秋"、"啃秋"（借西瓜、香瓜等瓜果祛除暑日积蓄在体内的湿气）等习俗。

During the period of Start of Autumn, there is a folk custom of offering sacrifices to the Earth God and celebrating the harvest. In ancient times, after Start of Autumn harvest, people would choose a lucky day to perform rituals. On the one hand, they would worship

God and thank the ancestors for their blessing; on the other hand, they would try the newly-harvested rice and grain to celebrate their hard-won harvest. In addition, there are also folk customs such as "putting on autumn fat" (for example, eating meat), "biting autumn" and "gnawing autumn" (eating watermelon, muskmelon and other fruits to dispel the summer heat accumulated in the body during the hot days) on the day of Start of Autumn.

处 暑
End of Heat

扫码看视频

处暑是二十四节气的第十四个节气，也是秋季的第二个节气。处暑，即为"出暑"，这时三伏已过或接近尾声，在每年公历的 8 月 22、23 或 24 日交节。这期间，天气虽热，但气温已呈下降趋势。处暑是反映气温变化的一个节气，这一节气意味着进入气象意义上的秋天。处暑后冷空气会时常影响我国，每每风雨过后，人们都会感到降温明显。

End of Heat is the 14th solar term of the 24 solar terms and the second solar term of autumn. End of Heat, also known as "out of summer", starts from August 22nd, 23rd or 24th each year in the solar calendar. It is the end or near the end of the Dog Days. In this period, although the weather is hot, temperature has shown a downward trend. It is a solar term that reflects the change of temperature, and it also means entering autumn in the meteorological term. After this solar term, cold air would constantly affect our country and after the winds and rain, people will apparently feel the weather's cooling.

民俗传统
Folk Customs

民间有处暑吃鸭子的传统，因为鸭肉味甘咸、性凉，具有滋阴养胃、利水消肿的作用，对久病者有很好的食补效果。在我国广东、广西地区，处暑有煎药茶的习俗。人们会去药店配制药茶，然后在家煎药茶，寓意入秋要吃点"苦"。在有些地区，民众会把河灯放在江河湖海之中，任它们漂流。放河灯表达了民众对逝去亲人的思念之情，以及对生活安康的祝福。

There is a folk tradition of eating duck during End of Heat, because the duck meat tastes sweet, salty, and is cool in nature, with the effect of nourishing Yin and the stomach, and reducing swelling. It has a good tonifying effect on those who have been ill for a long time. There is a custom of decocting medicinal tea in Guangdong and Guangxi provinces. People will go to the pharmacy to get the prescriptions, and then make medicinal tea at home, intentionally to eat some "bitterness" in autumn. In some areas, people will put lanterns in rivers, lakes and seas, and let them float freely. The release of river lanterns expresses the public's condolences for the deceased loved ones and their blessings for the well-being of life.

农事活动
Farming Activities

在这个节气里，南方的人们要继续做好蔬菜瓜果的抗旱、防台风工作。在台风、暴雨后加强培育管理，并及时抢种速生蔬菜，加强病虫害防治。例如，对柑橘的管理，继续以抗旱、抗台风、促进果实生长和促进秋梢生长为中心，加强对锈壁虱、潜叶蛾等害虫的防治，警惕炭疽病、溃疡病的发生，追肥促梢、喷施叶面肥壮叶。而对杨梅

的管理，则以抗旱、抗台风、控秋梢、促进花芽分化为中心，做好卷叶蛾、蓑蛾等害虫的防治工作。

In this solar term, people in southern China need to continue to prevent vegetables and fruits from the damage of droughts and typhoons. After the typhoon and rainstorm, people will strengthen cultivation and management, and timely rush to plant fast-growing vegetables, and strengthen the prevention and control of diseases and pests. For example, for citrus, people will continue to focus on drought resistance, typhoons resistance, fruit growth promotion and autumn shoot growth. They will also strengthen the prevention and control of rusty ticks, leaf latent moths and other pests, and guard against the occurrence of anthrax and canker disease. People also need to add fertilizer to promote shoots growth, and spray the foliar fertilizer to strengthen the leaves. Fot waxberry, efforts are focused on drought resistance, typhoon resistance, and autumn shoot control and the promotion of flower bud differentiation, as well as the prevention and control of leaf curling moths, ghost moths and other pests.

结尾
Ending

处暑是夏末秋初的过渡，它是一段沉淀的时光。

End of Heat ushers in the transition from late summer to early autumn. It is a time of calming down.

白 露

White Dew

扫码看视频

"蒹葭苍苍，白露为霜。"《诗经》这句诗里的"白露"即指二十四节气中的白露。白露是入秋后的第三个节气，于每年公历 9 月 7、8 或 9 日交节。此时天气转凉，夜晚空气中的水蒸气常在草木上凝成白色的露珠，白露由此得名。

"Sere sere reeds grow, White Dew frosts slow". White Dew in the poem of *The Book of Songs* (*Shi Jing*) refers to one of the 24 solar terms with the same name. White Dew, the third solar term after autumn, starts from September 7th, 8th or 9th every year in the solar calendar. The air turns cool, and the vapor in the air often condenses into white dew on plants at night, hence the name of White Dew.

民俗传统
Folk Customs

在白露这天，不同地区有不同的风俗。南京人要在这天品尝白露茶，这个时节的茶叶既不像春茶那么鲜嫩，也不像夏茶那么干苦。有些地方有吃"三白"（例如白萝卜、白绒乌骨鸡、白豆腐等"白色"食物）的习俗。它们大多具有滋阴、润肺、生津等作用，适合在秋天食用。福州有在白露吃龙眼的传统，据说在这天吃龙眼可以起到上佳的滋补作用。

During White Dew, different regions have different customs. People in Nanjing are used to drinking White Dew tea on this day. The tea of this season is not as fresh as spring tea, and not as dry and bitter as summer tea. In some regions, there is a custom of eating "Three Whites", which includes foods like white radish, white-feather silky chicken, white Tofu and other "white" foods. These foods are predominantly known for nourishing Yin, moistening the lungs, and generating body fluids, making them particularly suitable for consumption during the autumn season. People in Fuzhou has a tradition of eating longans on White Dew, as they believe eating longan at this time would have very good tonic effects.

农事活动
Farming Activities

中国古人根据对大自然的观察，将白露分为三候："一候鸿雁来，二候玄鸟归，三候群鸟养羞。"意思是说白露时节，鸿雁与燕子等候鸟南飞避寒，百鸟开始贮存干果粮食以备过冬。这会儿农民也忙着收获庄稼，正所谓"抢秋抢秋，不抢就丢"。

Based on the observation on nature, the ancient Chinese people divided White Dew into three periods or three phases. "The first period welcomes back the swan geese; the second would see the return of swallows; and during the last period, birds would start to store." It

means that during this solar term, migratory birds such as swan geese and swallows would fly south to avoid the cold, and the birds begin to store nuts and grain for the winter. Farmers are also busy harvesting. As the saying goes, "Grab the autumn, grab harvest, or you will lose it."

生活提示
Life Tips

　　白露意味着由热转凉，随寒气增长，万物逐渐成熟、衰落。白露时节，正是中国各地大忙之时。在白露节气中要预防鼻腔疾病、哮喘病和支气管炎的发生，饮食养生以生津润肺为主，宜多吃生津润肺的蔬菜和水果。

White Dew means the transition from heat to cool. Things ripen or fall as the weather gets colder and colder. It is a busy season for farmers all over China. During this time, we should prevent nasal diseases, asthma and bronchitis diseases, and it is advisable to eat more vegetables and fruits that can promote production of body fluid and nourish lungs.

结尾
Ending

　　"白露白茫茫，无被不上床。"白露意味着真正的秋天已经来到，提醒大家增添衣物，注意防寒保暖。

"White Dew spreads its vast whiteness. Without a quilt, one cannot go to bed." The real autumn has come. So don't forget to put on more clothes.

秋　分
Autumn Equinox

扫码看视频

　　"暑退秋澄气转凉，日光夜色两均长。"这就是秋分，我们传统农历二十四节气中的第十六个节气，一般在每年公历的9月22、23或24日交节。在这一天昼夜达到平分，从这之后昼短夜长的趋势就会变得越来越明显。

Summer receding, autumn coming, the weather turns cool, and day and night are equivalently long. This is the Autumn Equinox, the 16th of the 24 solar terms of the traditional lunar calendar. It starts generally from September 22nd, 23rd or 24th in the solar calendar. On this day, the day and night are equal, after which the trend of shorter days and longer nights will become more and more obvious.

三秋时节
Three Autumn Periods

董仲舒在《春秋繁露》中说："秋分者，阴阳相半也，故昼夜均而寒暑平。"古代把秋季分为孟秋、仲秋、季秋三部分，而秋分正处于仲秋，所谓平分秋色是也。在气候方面，秋分有三候："一候雷始收声，二候蛰虫坯户，三候水始涸。"这依次是指秋分之后阴气渐浓，蛰居的虫子开始用泥土封闭自己的巢穴，而从这以后北方地区降水会变少，我国大部分地区都可以感受到浓浓的秋意。

Dong Zhongshu said in *Luxuriant Dew of the Spring and Autumn Annals* that "The Autumn Equinox sees the equal of Yin and Yang, so day and night are equal, and cold and heat are balanced." In ancient times, autumn was divided into three phases, called Mengqiu, Zhongqiu, and Jiqiu. Autumn Equinox is in the middle of autumn. In terms of climate, Autumn Equinox has three phases: In the first phase, the thunder begins to cease. In the second phase, hibernating insects begin to close their burrows. In the third phase, the water begins to dry up. All of them suggest that after the Autumn Equinox, the Yin energy gradually intensifies, and hibernating insects begin to seal their nests with mud. After this, the precipitation in the northern region will also decrease, and the features of autumn can be detected in most parts of China.

秋收盛宴
Autumn Harvest Feast

秋分这一天，岭南地区的人们要吃汤圆，而且要把不用包心的十多个或二三十个汤圆煮好，用细竹叉扦着置于田边地坎，名曰粘雀嘴。在岭南地区，一些农村还有"秋分吃秋菜"的习俗。"秋菜"是一种野苋菜，逢秋分那天，当地人便外出采摘秋菜。采回的秋菜一般与鱼片一起蒸煮，名曰"秋汤"。岭南地区农村还有挨家挨户送秋牛图的习俗。在二开红纸或黄纸上印上全年农历节气，还要印上农夫耕田图样，名曰"秋牛图"。

On Autumn Equinox, people in Lingnan area will eat glutinous rice puddings. They will also cook a dozen or thirty glutinous rice balls and place them on the ridge of the field with thin bamboo strips, which is to "stick sparrow's beak". In some rural areas in the Lingnan area, there is still the custom of "eating autumn vegetables on the Autumn Equinox".

"Autumn vegetable" is a kind of wild amaranth. On Autumn Equinox, the whole village goes to pick "autumn vegetables". The harvested "autumn vegetables" are usually boiled in the soup with fish fillets, which is called "autumn soup". In Lingnan rural area, there is a custom of sending pictures of autumn cattle (Qiu Niu Tu) from house to house. The autumn cattle picture is printed on a sheet of A1 size red paper or yellow paper, with a solar term calender of the year and also a pattern of farmers ploughing the fields on it.

结尾
Ending

金黄色、绿色、红色……每一种颜色都代表着收成。春华秋实的背后是稼穑艰难，让我们向数以亿计的农民致敬。秉承天地"粮"心，珍惜每一粒粮食，是对农民劳动成果的最好尊重。

Golden, green, red... all colors represent the harvest. Behind the spring flowers and autumn fruits is the hard work of farmers. Thus, we should pay tribute to hundreds of millions of farmers. Adhering to the heart of the "grain" of heaven and earth, cherishing every grain is the best way to respect the hard work of farmers.

寒 露
Cold Dew

扫码看视频

　　寒露，在每年公历的 10 月 7、8 或 9 日交节。从字面上说，"寒"是指寒冷的意思，"露"为水汽凝结成露水，说明到了寒露时节，便真正步入秋天。此时气温有了明显下降，太阳到达黄经 195°，昼短夜长，早晚温差很大，保暖防寒成了重要的工作。《月令七十二候集解》上也说："九月节，露气寒冷，将凝结也。"可见到了该节气，温度比白露时更低，地面的露水更冷，快要凝结成霜了。常见的物候现象是大雁南飞，菊花盛开，很多动物都潜藏起来不见踪影。

　　Cold Dew starts from October 7th, 8th or 9th in the solar calendar. Literally, "Han" means cold, and "Lu" means dew formed by condensed water vapor. Cold Dew marks the real coming of the autumn season. There's a significant drop in temperature. The sun reaches 195 degrees celestial longitude. Days are short and nights are long, and there will be great temperature differences between the morning and evening. Therefore, keeping warm and preventing cold became important. *Explanations of the Seventy-Two Seasonal Divisions of*

the Monthly Ordinance also said that "In the ninth month, the dew becomes cold and is about to freeze." It can be seen that the temperature around Cold Dew is lower than that of White Dew. The dew on the ground is colder and nearly condenses into frost. The common phenomenon around this time is wild geese flying south, chrysanthemums blooming, and many animals hiding themselves.

喝菊花酒
Drinking Chrysanthemum Wine

一般人们会喝以菊花为原料酿造而成、味道甘美的菊花酒，据说喝菊花酒有延年益寿的功效。

Generally, people will drink chrysanthemum wine, which is made from chrysanthemum as raw material and tastes sweet. It is said that drinking chrysanthemum wine has the effect of prolonging life.

登高赏秋
Climbing Mountain to Enjoy the Autumn View

由于寒露临近重阳节，很多人会选择去爬山，登高欣赏美景，这也给在外的游子提供了一个思念家乡的空闲时间。

As it is close to the Double Ninth Festival, many people will choose to climb mountains to enjoy the beautiful scenery. It's usually a time that would arouse the homesickness of the wanderers.

吃重阳糕
Eating Double Ninth Cake

重阳糕也叫花糕，各地的做法不一样，但都代表着步步高升之意，因为糕与"高"同音，吃了重阳糕象征已经登过高山，将来好运将节节攀升。

The Double Ninth Cake is also called flower cake. The cakes vary from place to place, but they all carry the wish for progress and promotion. Because "cake" (gāo) has the same pronunciation as "high" (gāo) in Chinese, eating it symbolizes that you have climbed the mountain and good luck will increase in the future.

结尾
Ending

　　寒露是一年中比较靠后的一个节气，不仅代表着天气转寒，也提醒我们想要过一个舒适的、暖心的冬天，现在就该做好养生的准备啦。

　　Cold Dew is a solar term that comes later in a year. It not only means the cold weather, but also reminds us that if we want to live a comfortable and heart-warming winter, it's time to prepare for seasonal health care now.

霜　降
Frost's Descent

扫码看视频

　　霜降是中国传统二十四节气中的第十八个节气。霜降期间，气候由凉向寒过渡，所以霜降的来临意味着"寒秋"的开始。霜降一般是在每年公历的 10 月 23 日或 24 日交节，太阳到达黄经 210°。霜降是秋季的最后一个节气，是秋季到冬季的过渡节气。晚秋地面散热多，温度有时下降到零摄氏度以下，空气中的水蒸气在地面或植物上直接凝结，形成细微的冰针，有的成为六角形的霜花，色白且结构疏松。

　　Frost's Descent is the 18th solar term of the 24 traditional Chinese solar terms. During Frost's Descent, the climate changes from cool to cold, so the coming of Frost's Descent means the beginning of "cold autumn". Frost's Descent usually starts from October 23rd or 24th of the solar calendar. When the sun reaches the celestial longitude of 210 degrees, it is Frost's Descent of the 24 solar terms. Frost's Descent is the last solar term of autumn and marks the transitional period from autumn to winter. In late autumn, there is a lot of heat dissipating on the ground, and the temperature sometimes drops to below 0℃. Water vapor in the air directly condenses on the ground or plants to form tiny ice needles, some of which become hexagonal frost flowers, which are white and have a loose structure.

霜降

晴日生霜
Frost Condenses in Sunny Days

霜降恰逢晚秋，天气渐冷，开始有霜。霜，只能在晴天形成，人说"浓霜猛太阳"，就是这个道理。气象学上，一般把秋季出现的第一次霜叫作"早霜"，而把春季出现的最后一次霜称为"晚霜"。也有把早霜叫作"菊花霜"的，因为此时菊花盛开。

Frost's Descent happens in late autumn when the weather gets colder and frost begins to appear. Frost can only form on clear days, and the saying "a heavy frost follows a fierce sun" encapsulates this principle. In meteorology, the first occurrence of frost in the autumn is commonly referred to as "early frost". Conversely, the last frost of the spring season is known as "late frost". The term "chrysanthemum frost" is also used to describe the early frost because it coincides with the blooming of chrysanthemums.

霜降美味
Delicacies in Frost's Descent

谈到霜降，那美食可不能缺席。在我国一些地方，霜降吃红柿子，可以起到润肺、补虚、解酒、止咳的效果。白萝卜也不能少，山东有句农谚"处暑高粱，白露谷，霜降到了拔萝卜"，强调了不同时节不同食物的重要性。

When it comes to Frost's Descent, you can't miss the delicious food. In some places of our country, during Frost's Descent, we should eat red persimmon, which can play the effect of moistening the lung, restoring the deficiency, dispelling effects of alcohol and relieving cough. White radish is an essential vegetable in the diet. There is a well-known agricultural proverb in Shandong that goes "Sorghum after End of Heat, millet after White Dew, and radishes after Frost's Descent," highlighting the importance of different foods according to the seasonal changes.

霜寒多疾
Common Diseases in Frost's Descent

霜降节气是慢性胃炎和十二指肠溃疡复发的高峰期。老年人也极容易患上"老寒腿"（膝关节骨性关节炎的毛病），慢性支气管炎也容易复发或加重。这时应该多吃些秋梨、苹果、洋葱、芥菜等。

Frost's Descent is the peak period of chronic gastritis and duodenal ulcer recurrence. The elderly are also very prone to suffer from "old cold legs" (knee osteoarthritis), and chronic bronchitis is also easy to relapse or aggravate. At this time, one should eat more pears, apples, onions, mustard, etc.

结尾
Ending

霜降，如同我们人一生中在不同阶段所遭受的挫折和打击，它给我们带来寒冷和孤独，却也给我们带来成长和希望。当五彩缤纷的叶子从树梢飘落，霜降大地，是告别，亦是相逢。当曾经灿烂的生命跳完最后一支舞蹈，风落木归山，是结束，也是开始。

Frost's Descent, much like the setbacks and blows we encounter at different stages of our lives, brings us coldness and solitude. Yet, it also brings us growth and hope. As the colorful leaves fall from the treetops and the frost blankets the earth, it signifies not only a farewell but also an encounter. When once radiant lives finish their final dances and the wind carries the fallen leaves back to the mountains, it marks an end but also a new beginning.

立　　冬
Start of Winter

扫码看视频

　　立冬与立春、立夏、立秋合称"四立"，在古代社会中是个重要的节日。劳动了一年的人们，在立冬这一天要休息一下，犒赏一家人一年来的辛苦，故有谚语说"立冬补冬，补嘴空"。现在让我们一起来了解一下立冬以及立冬期间的农业、养生以及民间习俗等活动吧。

　　Start of Spring, Start of Summer, Start of Autumn, Start of Winter, all together are called "the Four Starts". Start of Winter is a major festival in ancient times. People who have worked for a year shall have a rest on this day and reward themselves for the hard work during a year. So there is a saying that "Beginning of Winter, Supplement for Winter. Have some nutritious foods and fortify the body." Now let's take a look at Start of Winter and the activities of agriculture, health preservation and folk customs during the solar term.

　　立冬，是二十四节气中的第十九个节气，于每年公历11月7日或8日交节。立，建始也；冬，万物收藏也。立冬是季节类节气，表示自此进入了冬季，生气开始闭蓄，万物进入休养生息状态，气候也由秋季向冬季渐变。

　　Start of Winter, the 19th solar term of the year, starts from November 7th or 8th in the solar calendar. "Li", means the beginning; winter is the time when all things tend to store and conserve their energy. Start of Winter is a seasonal solar term, which means that from then on, things go into dormancy and enter the state of rest and recuperation. The climate also changes from autumn to winter.

秋收冬种
Harvest in Autumn and Planting in Winter

　　这时节正是秋收冬种的大好时段，立冬前后，我国大部分地区降水显著减少。东北地区大地封冻，农林作物进入越冬期；江南正忙着抢种晚茬冬麦，抓紧移栽油菜。相比之下，在华南地区，特别是广东和广西地区，气候较为温和，这使得那里的农业时间表有所不同。俗话说"立冬正是种麦时"，反映了华南地区的农业智慧。

　　During this season, it is the optimal time for autumn harvest and winter planting. Around the time of Start of Winter, precipitation in most parts of China significantly decreases. The northeastern region experiences the freezing of the soil, and agricultural and forestry crops enter their winter dormancy period. Meanwhile, in the areas south of the Yangtze River, farmers are busy planting the late sown winter wheat and hastily transplanting rape seedling. In contrast, the southern region of China, particularly in the Guangdong and Guangxi areas, experiences a milder climate that allows for a different agricultural schedule. The saying "It is the perfect time to plant wheat at Start of Winter" reflects south China's agricultural wisdom.

立冬时节如何养生
How to Keep Healthy during Start of Winter

唐代著名医学家孙思邈说："冬月不宜清早出深夜归，冒犯寒威。"立冬后，建议早睡晚起，保证充足的睡眠。另外，立冬后，人的免疫力和体质会下降，散步、慢跑、瑜伽等运动会是不错的选择。

According to Sun Simiao, a famous medical scientist of the Tang Dynasty, in winter, it is not advisable to leave early in the morning and return late at night due to the harsh cold. After Start of Winter, it is recommended to go to bed early and get up late to ensure adequate sleep. In addition, after Start of Winter, people's immunity and physical fitness will decline. Walking, jogging, and yoga are all suitable forms of exercise for this period.

立冬吃饺子
Eating Dumplings on Start of Winter

立冬是秋冬季节之交，故"交"子之时的饺子不能不吃。并且水饺外形似耳朵，古时人们认为吃了它，冬天耳朵就不会受冻。也有人说饺子像元宝，寓意来年财源广进。立冬吃饺子是对传承了数千年的中华习俗的一种延续。

Start of Winter comes at the turn of autumn and winter, so you can't miss eating dumplings at that time. And dumplings' shape looks like ears. People in ancient times believed that eating them would protect their ears from the cold in winter. Some people say dumplings are like gold ingots, meaning the next year's wealth. Eating dumplings on Start of Winter is a continuation of thousands of years of Chinese customs.

结尾
Ending

　　秋收冬藏。告别秋天，才能更好地遇见冬天。在这严肃又寂寥的表象之下，其实是一份释怀和温暖。

　　Harvest in autumn and storage in winter. As we bid farewell to autumn, we can better encounter winter. Beneath the seemingly stern and desolate appearance of winter lies a sense of relief and warmth.

小 雪
Minor Snow

扫码看视频

小雪，交节时间为每年公历 11 月 22 或 23 日。小雪是反映气温与降水变化趋势的节气。这个节气之所以叫小雪，是因为"雪"是寒冷天气的产物，且这个节气期间"气候寒未深且降水未大"。

Minor Snow starts from November 22nd or 23rd in the solar calendar. Minor Snow reflects the changing trend of temperature and rainfall. The reason why this solar term is called Xiaoxue is that "snow" is the product of cold weather, and during this solar term, the climate is not very cold and the precipitation is not heavy.

冬腊风腌，蓄以御冬
Cure Meats for Winter Treats

小雪时节气温急剧下降，天气变得干燥，是腌制腊肉的好时候。一些农家开始动手做香肠、腊肉，把多余的肉类用传统方法储备起来，等到春节时正好享用美食。很多地方都有冬季吃腊肉的习俗，尤其是南方城市，更是对腊味情有独钟。

During Minor Snow, the temperature drops sharply, and the weather becomes dry, which is the best time to cure meats. Some rural households start to make sausages and cured meats, preserving extra meat in traditional methods to enjoy during the Chinese New Year. Many regions have the tradition of eating cured meats in winter, especially in southern cities, where there is a particular fondness for the flavors of cured meats.

结尾
Ending

小雪时节，愿你我，都能与一场初雪相遇，有些许温暖入心！

In Minor Snow, may you and I both meet the first snow and feel some warmth in our hearts!

扫码看视频

大　雪
Major Snow

大雪，顾名思义，雪量大。大雪是二十四节气中的第二十一个节气，冬季的第三个节气，交节时间为每年公历 12 月 6、7 或 8 日。大雪节气标志着仲冬时节正式开始。关于大雪，你了解多少呢？跟我们一起来看看吧！

Major Snow, as the name suggests, means a huge amount of snow. It is the 21st solar term and the third solar term of winter, which starts from December 6th, 7th or 8th in the solar calendar. Major Snow marks the beginning of the midwinter season. How much do you know about Major Snow? Just follow us and have a look!

气候特征
Climate Characteristics

大雪时节，中国大部分地区已进入冬季，最低温度降到了零摄氏度或以下，在冷暖空气交汇的地区会降大雪。此时，黄河流域一带已渐有积雪，而在更北的地方，则大雪纷飞了。

During Major Snow, most parts of China have entered the winter, and the lowest temperature has dropped to 0℃ or below. Heavy snow will fall in areas where warm and cold air collide. At that time, there is already accumulated snow along the Yellow River, while in the farther north, snow becomes heavy.

农事活动
Farming Activities

从小雪节气到大雪节气，雪量不断加大。一般来讲雪下得越多越好，雪对于来年地表水分的积蓄起着关键性的作用。而地面的积雪，一可以给冬小麦保温保湿，防止冬季干吹风；二可以储存来年作物生长所需的水分；三能冻死土壤表面的一些虫卵，减少病虫害的发生。但雪太大，也会对一些农业设施产生不利影响。

Snow normally increases from Minor Snow to Major Snow. The more snow, the better, for it plays a key role in the accumulation of surface moisture in the coming year. First, the

snow on the ground can keep warm and moisturize winter wheat and prevent dry winds in winter; second, it can store the water needed for crop growth in the coming year; third, it can freeze some insect eggs on the surface of the soil and reduce the occurrence of pests and diseases. But if the snow is too heavy, it will also have some negative impacts on agriculture facilities.

民俗传统
Folk Customs

腌肉、打雪仗、赏雪景都是大雪节气的民俗。老南京有句俗话，叫作"小雪腌菜，大雪腌肉"。此时，很多人家的门口和窗台上都会挂上腌肉、香肠、咸鱼等腌制品，形成一道诱人的风景。如果此时恰逢天降大雪，人们都会热衷于在冰天雪地里打一场雪仗。

Pickling meat, having a snowball fight and viewing the snow are all the folk customs during Major Snow. There is an old saying in Nanjing, "Pickle vegetables on Minor Snow, and pickle meat on Major Snow." At this time, many households would hang pickled meat, sausage, salted fish, etc. at their doorstep and windowsill, forming an attractive scenery. If snow falls, people will be keen to have a snowball fight despite the freezing weather.

冬　　至
Winter Solstice

扫码看视频

冬至是二十四节气中的第二十二个，在每年公历的 12 月 21、22 或 23 日交节，也是现在公历年中最后一个节气。唐代诗人白居易曾写过一首诗《邯郸冬至夜思家》："邯郸驿里逢冬至，抱膝灯前影伴身。想得家中夜深坐，还应说着远行人。"他借冬至表达了对家人的思念之情。

Winter Solstice is the 22nd of the 24 solar terms, which starts from December 21st, 22nd or 23rd every year of the solar calendar, and also the last solar term in the current solar calendar. Bai Juyi of the Tang Dynasty once wrote a poem "Thinking of Home on Winter Solstice Night at Handan."

At roadside inn I pass Winter Solstice Day.

Clasping my knees, with my shadow in company.

I think, till dead of night my family would stay,

And talk about the poor lonely wayfaring me.

He took Winter Solstice as a special occasion to express thoughts of his family.

冬至大如年
Winter Solstice Is As Important as the Chinese New Year

"如果冬天来了，春天还会远吗？"相比其他节气，冬至具有更重要的地位。在民间，冬至有"冬节""长至节""亚岁"的称谓，民谚中更是有"冬至大如年"的说法。

"If winter comes, can spring be far behind?" Winter Solstice is different from other solar terms and considered more important. Folks also call it "Winter Festival", "Changzhi Festival" or "Ya Sui". There is also a saying that winter Solstice is as important as the Chinese New Year.

冬至为始
Winter Solstice Is the Beginning

冬至的名字大有来头，古书里解释："至有三义，一者阴极之至，二者阳气始至，三者日行南至，故谓至。"对于古代的农耕生活来说，从冬至开始，阴气降低，阳气回升，象征白天变长，因此古人认为，冬至代表下一个循环的开始，是大吉之日。所以周代以冬十一月为正月，以冬至为岁首过新年。因此冬至也被称为"冬节"。

Winter Solstice has profound meanings. According to ancient books, "Zhi" can be understood from three aspects. One is the arrival of the extreme of Yin; the second is the beginning of the onset of Yang; and the third is that the direct sunshine arrives at the

southernmost position. For people leading the ancient farming life, the Yin energy decreased and the Yang energy rose since Winter Solstice, symbolizing that the day became longer. Therefore, the ancients believed that Winter Solstice made the day an auspicious one representing the beginning of the next cycle. So, in the Zhou Dynasty, November was the first month, and Winter Solstice was the beginning of the New Year, hence also the name "Winter Festival".

冬至阳生
Yang Energy Grows in Winter Solstice

冬至这天象征着阳气之始，在饮食方面也与此相呼应。在冬至这天，北方人一般吃饺子，而南方人则习惯吃汤圆和馄饨。同时冬至也是冬补之时，可适当选用当归、地黄、枸杞、山药等升举阳气之物以达到防病强身的保健作用。

Winter Solstice symbolizes the beginning of the Yang energy, which is embodied in the food. On this day, people in northern China generally eat dumplings, while those in southern China eat tangyuan and wontons. Therefore, Winter Solstice is also a good time for nourishment in winter. People can select some medicines full of Yang energy such as Chinese angelica roots, rehmannia roots, goji berries, and yam for nourishment, aiming to prevent diseases and promote health.

结尾
Ending

其实，无论是古代还是现代，冬至的到来都意味着一个崭新的起点，人生正在奔向更加灿烂的明天。

Indeed, whether in ancient times or the modern era, the arrival of Winter Solstice signifies that life is embarking on a fresh beginning. We are heading for a brighter tomorrow.

小　寒
Minor Cold

扫码看视频

　　小寒是二十四节气中的第二十三个节气，是干支历子月的结束以及丑月的起始，在公历 1 月 5、6 或 7 日交节。"小寒，十二月节。月初寒尚小，故云。月半则大矣。"小寒节气名字由此而来。下面我们来一起了解一下过小寒的传统习俗。

　　Minor Cold is the 23rd solar term in the 24 solar terms. It marks the end of the eleventh month and the beginning of the twelfth month in Chinese lunar calendar, which starts from January 5th, 6th or 7th in the solar calendar. "The cold at the beginning of the twelfth month is minor, hence the name of Minor Cold. And it gradually becomes major around the middle of the month." Let's take a look at the traditional customs of Minor Cold.

探梅
Wintersweet Appreciation

　　小寒时蜡梅已开，红梅含苞待放，挑选有梅花的绝佳风景地，细细观赏，鼻中有孤雅幽香，神志也会随之清爽振奋。

　　During Minor Cold, the wintersweet is already in bloom, while the red plum flowers are in early puberty. If you find a place with the best scenery of wintersweet for appreciation, your nose will be filled with fragrance that refreshes your mind.

冰戏
Ice Games

　　我国北方的各省，入冬后天寒地坼，结冰期会非常久，动辄从 11 月起，直到次年 4 月。河面结冰厚实，冰上交通工具可用爬犁。冰面特厚的地方，有时会设有冰床，供行人来玩耍，也有穿冰鞋在冰面竞走的，古代的时候称之为"冰戏"。

　　In northern China, the weather is freezing after entering winter, with a long ice period which usually ranges from November to April in the next year. Rivers are thickly frozen, and one can use a plow as a vehicle. In places with thick ice surfaces, there are ice beds set up for

pedestrians to play on sometimes. People can put on ice skates and compete in races across the ice surfaces, an activity that was referred to as "ice games" in ancient times.

腊祭
La Sacrifice

　　小寒是腊月的节气，由于古人会在农历十二月份举行合祀众神的腊祭，因此把腊祭所在的十二月叫作腊月。"腊"的本义是"接"，取新旧交接的意思。腊祭为我国古代祭祀习俗之一，远在先秦时期就已经有这个习俗了。

　　Minor Cold is a solar term in the 12th month in the Chinese lunar calendar (also known as La Month in Chinese). In ancient times, people would hold a sacrifice ceremony in worship of gods in the 12th month, hence the name of La Sacrifice. The original meaning of "La" is "transition", which means the transition from the old to new time. La Sacrifice is one of the ancient sacrificial customs in China, which dates back to the pre-Qin period.

准备年货
New Year Goods Preparation

小寒节气是二十四节气中的第二十三个节气，小寒时节到了之后，也就意味着距离春节已经不远了。因此，小寒的时候很多地方的年味渐浓，家家户户都已经开始忙着写春联、剪窗花，赶集买年画、彩灯、鞭炮等，陆续为春节做准备。

When Minor Cold, the 23rd solar term of Chinese 24 solar terms, falls, the Chinese New Year is right around the corner. Therefore, the Spring Festival atmosphere is getting thicker in many places when Minor Cold arrives, and every household has been busy writing Spring Festival couplets, making paper-cutting window decorations, and buying New Year paintings, festive lanterns, firecrackers, and so on, in preparation for the Chinese New Year.

结尾
Ending

小寒，冬季中最美的时节。这时的世界冰凌未尽，春讯未迟，有一番别样的风景。

Minor Cold is the most gorgeous period in winter. At this time, the world remains in the grip of lingering frost, and spring is on the way, presenting a different scenery to the world.

大　寒
Major Cold

扫码看视频

大寒，是二十四节气中的最后一个节气，在每年公历 1 月 20 日或 21 日交节。大寒同小寒一样，也是表示天气寒冷程度的节气，大寒就是天气寒冷到极致的意思。

Major Cold is the last solar term in the 24 solar terms, which falls on January 20th or 21st in the solar calendar. Major Cold, like Minor Cold, is also a solar term that represents the degree of coldness, meaning that the weather is extremely cold.

气象特征
Meteorological Features

根据我国长期以来的气象记录，在北方地区大寒节气是没有小寒冷的，但对于南方大部分地区来说，最冷的时候是在大寒节气。大寒在岁终，冬去春来，大寒一过，又开始一个新的轮回。

According to the long-term meteorological records of our country, in northern China, it is warmer in Major Cold than in Minor Cold, but for most parts of southern China, it is the coldest in Major Cold. Major Cold is at the end of the lunar year, marking that winter will leave and spring will arrive. As soon as Major Cold passes, a new cycle begins.

农事活动
Farming Activities

大寒节气里，各地农活依旧很少。北方地区的老百姓多忙于积肥、堆肥，为开春做准备。这时期由于寒潮南下频繁，农业上要加强牲畜和越冬作物的防寒防冻，并根据农作物属性，因地制宜选择农作物品种。南方地区则仍需加强小麦及其他作物的田间管理。

During Major Cold, there is still very little farm work. People in the north are mostly busy collecting and composting fertilizers for the coming spring. During this period, due to the frequent cold wave to the south, it is necessary to strengthen the cold and frost prevention

of livestock and overwintering crops, and select crop varieties according to local conditions and crop attributes. Field management of wheat and other crops still need to be strengthened in the south.

习俗传统
Folk Customs

　　大寒时节，人们开始忙着除旧布新，腌制年肴，准备年货，因为中国人最重要的节日——春节就要到了。有时大寒期间，还有一个对于北方人来讲非常重要的日子——腊八。在这一天，人们用五谷杂粮加上花生、栗子、红枣、莲子等熬成一锅香甜美味的腊八粥。

　　During Major Cold, people are busy replacing the old decorations with the new, pickling New Year dishes and preparing New Year's goods, because the Chinese New Year, the most important festival for Chinese people, is coming. Sometimes in the meantime, there is a very important day for people in northern China—the Laba Festival. On this day, people boil the sweet and delicious Laba porridge with grains, peanuts, chestnuts, red dates and lotus seeds.

节气养生
Health Preservation Advice

本节气最需预防的是心脑血管病和肺气肿。另外，要加强体育锻炼，注意保暖。

In Major Cold, the most important diseases to prevent are cardiovascular and cerebrovascular diseases and emphysema. In addition, more physical exercise is needed, and more attention to keeping warm should be paid.

结尾
Ending

大寒是二十四节气之尾，其后紧随着除夕与春节，也是冬季即将结束之季。隐隐中已可感受到大地回春的迹象，但人们还是盼望着一场冬雪的到来。这样的三节相连，寓意为驱凶迎祥，万物复苏，春暖花开，让人们在新的一年里，在心中埋下一颗充满希望的种子。

Major Cold is the end of the 24 solar terms, followed by New Year's Eve and the Spring Festival, which is also the end of the winter season. Signs of the earth's rejuvenation can be faintly felt, but we still look forward to the arrival of a winter snow. Such a combination of Major Cold and two festivals means that the evil is expelled and the auspicious is welcomed. Everything revives, and the warm spring and blooming flowers are around the corner, planting a seed of hope in people's hearts in the new year.

诗词里的中国

China in Poetry

导　语
Introduction

诗词是文学的一种形式，也是中华文化传承的重要手段之一。它以简洁而富于意境的语言，深刻地反映了中国古代的社会现实、自然风貌以及人民的生活、文化、情感和思想。诗词如一条古老而富有生命力的河流，滋润着中华文化的根基；如一面镜子，反映出朝代的兴衰荣辱，映照出人性的善恶和情感的丰富；如一盏明亮的灯，照亮着人们迷茫时的心灵，指引着人们前行的方向。

Poetry is not only a form of literature, but also an important means of Chinese cultural inheritance. It deeply reflects the social reality, natural landscape, people's life, culture, emotions and thoughts of ancient China with simple language which is rich in artistic conception. Poetry, like an ancient and vibrant river, moistens the foundation of Chinese culture; like a mirror, it reflects the rise and fall of dynasties, as well as the good and evil of human nature and the richness of emotions; like a bright light, it illuminates people's hearts when they are confused and guides the way forward.

《诗经》是中华文化的瑰宝，是中国文学史上最早的诗歌总集，收集了从周初期至春秋中叶的诗歌 305 篇。《诗经》以《风》《雅》《颂》三种诗歌形式和"赋、比、兴"三种表现手法，反映了当时社会生活、风土人情、历史事件、自然景观、劳动生产、爱情婚姻等多方面的内容，展示了一个生动而真实的古代中国社会，是中国历史和文化的珍贵遗产。

The Book of Songs (*Shi Jing*), a treasure of Chinese culture, is the earliest collection of poems in the history of Chinese literature, collecting 305 poems from the early Zhou Dynasty to the middle of the Spring and Autumn Period. It reflects the social life, local customs, historical events, natural landscape, labor and production, love and marriage and other aspects in the poetic forms of "Feng" (Ballad), "Ya" (Court Hymn), and "Song" (Eulogy) by the

expression techniques of fu (narratives), bi (analogies) and xing (associations). It shows a vivid and real ancient Chinese society and is a precious heritage of Chinese history and culture.

唐诗是中国文学史上的一座丰碑，代表了中华诗歌的巅峰成就。不同时期的唐诗在风格和题材上有着显著的变化。初唐时期，诗歌摆脱了六朝的浮艳，显示出一种清新刚健的风骨，题材和内容从宫廷的奢靡转向广阔的社会生活和重大的政治问题。盛唐时期诗歌题材丰富多样，风格各异，有反映边塞军旅生活的边塞诗，有描绘宁静田园生活的田园诗；有"诗仙"李白充满浪漫主义色彩、想象丰富、意境深远的诗歌，也有"诗圣"杜甫反映社会现实、同情民间疾苦的诗歌。中唐时期因经历了安史之乱，诗歌主题更加现实，反映社会矛盾和民间疾苦的作品增多。晚唐时期随着国势衰微，诗歌多带有一种感伤和衰飒的基调。总的来说，唐诗数量众多，题材广泛，在艺术上也达到了极高的水平。

Tang poetry is a monument in the history of Chinese literature and represents the summit of Chinese poetry. Tang poetry in different periods has significant changes in style and subject matter. In the early Tang Dynasty, poetry got rid of the showiness of the six dynasties (220–589 CE) and showed a fresh and vigorous character. The subject matter and content changed from court extravagance to broad social life and major political issues. In the heyday of the Tang Dynasty poetry had various themes and styles. There were frontier poetry reflecting the military life of the frontier fortress, idyllic poetry describing the peaceful idyllic life, "the Immortal Poet" Li Bai's poems full of romanticism, rich imagination and profound artistic conception, and "the Poetry Sage" Du Fu's poems reflecting the social reality and sympathy for the people's sufferings. In the middle Tang Dynasty, due to the An-Shi (An Lushan-Shi Siming) Rebellion, the theme of poetry became more realistic, and the works reflecting social conflicts and people's sufferings increased. In the late Tang Dynasty, with the decline of national power, the poems were mostly sentimental. In general, Tang poetry is numerous with a wide range of themes, and has reached a very high level in art.

宋词是中国古代文化的重要组成部分，大多写景抒情，通过对自然景物的细腻描写来抒发个人情感，同时也表达作者对社会现象和人情世故的观察与思考，其特点是言简意赅、意境深远，常以寥寥数语引发深刻的共鸣。宋代词人苏轼、陆游、李清照等的词作，不仅描写了生活的琐碎和痛苦，也展现了对美好生活的向往和追求，反映了当时的社会风貌和人民情感。宋词语言优美，旋律悠扬，音乐性强，常常给人以美的享受。

Song ci poetry is an important part of ancient Chinese culture, mostly expressing personal feelings through the delicate description of natural scenery, and poets' observations and reflections on social phenomena and the ways of the world, characterized by being concise and comprehensive but with far-reaching artistic conception, resonating deeply with a few words. The lyrics of the Song Dynasty poets, such as Su Shi, Lu You and Li Qingzhao, not only describe the triviality and pain of life, but also show the yearning and pursuit of a better life, reflecting the social life and people's emotions at that time. Song lyrics are renowned for their beautiful language, melodious tunes, and strong musicality, often providing aesthetic pleasure to those who appreciate them.

元曲是中国文学史上一类独特的戏曲体裁，结合了音乐、舞蹈、戏剧等多种艺术形式，展示了元代社会的风貌和人民的情感。元曲中的剧情丰富，角色形象多样，内容涵盖了历史故事、神话传说、爱情故事等各个领域。元曲的语言生动活泼，韵律优美，极具表现力，常常通过对人性的探索，揭示理想与现实的矛盾。元曲不仅丰富了中国文学的形式和内容，也是中国戏曲文化的宝库。

Yuan verse is a unique drama genre in the history of Chinese literature, combining music, dance, drama and other artistic forms to show the social life and people's emotions of the Yuan Dynasty. The plots and characters in Yuan verse are diverse, covering historical stories, myths and legends, love stories and so on. The language of Yuan verse is lively, rhythmical and expressive. It often reveals the conflicts between ideal and reality through the exploration of human nature. Enriching the form and content of Chinese literature, Yuan verse is the treasure house of Chinese opera culture.

诗词是中华民族文化的精髓，具有极高的艺术价值、深刻的社会价值、广泛的文化交流价值，它不仅是中国文学的瑰宝，也是全人类共同的文化遗产。让我们走进"诗词里的中国"，感受中国古代文化的博大精深，更好地了解中国的历史和传统文化，体悟蕴含其中的人生智慧，提升自己的文学修养和审美情趣。

Poetry is the essence of Chinese national culture, possessing immense artistic value, profound social significance, and extensive cultural exchange value. It is not only a treasure of Chinese literature but also a shared cultural heritage of all humanity. Let's go into "China in Poetry" and feel the breadth and depth of ancient Chinese culture, to better understand Chinese history and traditional culture, the life wisdom contained therein, and improve our literary accomplishment and aesthetic taste.

诗经·卫风·木瓜
The Book of Songs·Wei Wind·Quince

扫码看视频

　　《诗经》共有《风》《雅》《颂》三个部分，其中《风》是指各地的民歌、民谣，大部分是黄河流域的民间乐歌，被称作"十五国风"，共 160 篇。《卫风》共有 10 篇，其中《木瓜》一诗广为传颂，但对其主旨有不同解释。从宋代朱熹起，"男女相互赠答说"开始流行，现代学者一般比较认同朱熹之说，并明确指出此诗是一首爱情诗。

　　Shi Jing, also known as *The Book of Songs*, comprises three sections—"Feng" (Ballad),

"Ya" (Court Hymn), and "Song" (Eulogy). Among them, "Feng" refers to folk songs and ballads from various regions, mostly folk songs from the Yellow River basin, known as the "15 Kingdoms Feng," totaling 160 poems. Within "Songs of Wei", there are ten poems, among which "quince (mugua)" is widely celebrated, but people have different interpretations for its main theme. Since the Song Dynasty, Zhu Xi's interpretation, which framed the poem as an exchange of gifts between men and women, gained popularity. Modern scholars generally agree with Zhu's view, specifically identifying this poem as a romantic one.

诗经 · 卫风 · 木瓜

投我以木瓜，报之以琼琚。

匪报也，永以为好也！

投我以木桃，报之以琼瑶。

匪报也，永以为好也！

投我以木李，报之以琼玖。

匪报也，永以为好也！

The Book of Songs · Songs of Wei · Quince

She throws a quince to me;

I give her a green jade

Not in return, you see,

But to show acquaintance made.

She throws a peach to me;

I give her a white jade

Not in return, you see,

But to show friendship made.

She throws a plum to me;

I give her jasper fair

Not in return, you see,

But to show love fore'er.

西周时期，贵族男女皆佩戴玉，玉既是身份的象征，又起到了装饰作用，因此玉在当时也成了男女互赠的重要物品。此诗是以一种假设的口吻，以"木瓜""木桃""木李"比喻微物，"琼琚""琼瑶""琼玖"比喻重宝，投桃报李，互赠礼物，是为了长以为好；所报之物再贵，也不能表达对心爱之人的浓情厚谊。在奇妙的字词之间可见抒情主人公的忠厚、深情。全诗句式重章复沓，语气由舒缓到急促，情感层层加深，诗韵自然而悠长。

During the Western Zhou period, both aristocratic men and women wore jade as a symbol of their status and for decorative purposes. Therefore, jade was an important item for men and women to exchange with each other. The poem "Quince" adopts a hypothetical tone, using "quince", "peach" and "plum" to metaphorically represent small things, and "qiongju (green jade)", "qiongyao (white jade)" and "qiongjiu (jasper fair)" to represent precious items. By exchanging gifts like peaches and plums, they sought lasting amity, but even the most valuable gifts could hardly convey the depth of affection for the loved one. Within the lyrical masterpiece, the sincerity and passion of the poet shine through the marvelous choice of words. The syntax of the whole poem is graceful and the structure is complex, with the tone gradually shifting from leisurely to urgent, and the emotions deepening layer by layer. The natural and enduring rhyme resonates profoundly.

这首诗通过描述赠予对方木瓜这一寻常事物，以真挚的情感和质朴的表达方式，深深地打动了读者。

This poem describes the simple act of giving each other a "Mugua (quince)". With its sincere emotions and simple articulation, it deeply touches its readers.

离骚（节选）
Sorrow after Departure (Excerpt)

扫码看视频

《离骚》是屈原的代表作，是一首充满政治激情和生命悲情的政治抒情诗。屈原"竭忠事君"，"谗人间之"，因而遭贬谪，被流放，最后投汨罗江而死。诗人屈原的"千丽句"终究敌不过上官、靳尚的"一谗言"，个人理想无法实现，"民生之多艰"，祖国陷入"路幽昧以险隘"的境地，爱国爱民的屈原陷入极度痛苦之中。

"Sorrow after Departure", the representative work of Qu Yuan, is a political lyric poem full of political passion and sorrow of life. Qu Yuan was loyal to "the Sacred One" but "alienated by slanderers", disgraced and sent into exile, and finally drowned himself in the Miluo River. His marvelous patriotic poems were eventually not worth the slanderous words of Shangguan Dafu and Jin Shang (two officials of Chu). Personal ideals could not be realized; "the people's livelihood was very difficult", the motherland got into a situation where "the path to the future is dangerous and bleak", all of which made the patriotic poet in great distress.

离骚（节选）

屈原

长太息以掩涕兮，哀民生之多艰。

余虽好修姱以鞿羁兮，謇朝谇而夕替。

既替余以蕙纕兮，又申之以揽茝。

亦余心之所善兮，虽九死其犹未悔。

怨灵修之浩荡兮，终不察夫民心。

众女嫉余之蛾眉兮，谣诼谓余以善淫。

固时俗之工巧兮，偭规矩而改错。

背绳墨以追曲兮，竞周容以为度。

忳郁邑余侘傺兮，吾独穷困乎此时也。

宁溘死以流亡兮，余不忍为此态也！

鸷鸟之不群兮，自前世而固然。

何方圜之能周兮，夫孰异道而相安？

屈心而抑志兮，忍尤而攘诟。

伏清白以死直兮，固前圣之所厚。

悔相道之不察兮，延伫乎吾将反。

回朕车以复路兮，及行迷之未远。

步余马于兰皋兮，驰椒丘且焉止息。

进不入以离尤兮，退将复修吾初服。

制芰荷以为衣兮，集芙蓉以为裳。

不吾知其亦已兮，苟余情其信芳。

高余冠之岌岌兮，长余佩之陆离。

芳与泽其杂糅兮，唯昭质其犹未亏。

忽反顾以游目兮，将往观乎四荒。

佩缤纷其繁饰兮，芳菲菲其弥章。

民生各有所乐兮，余独好修以为常。

虽体解吾犹未变兮，岂余心之可惩？

Sorrow after Departure (Excerpt)

Qu Yuan

I sigh and wipe away my tears, oh!

I'm grieved at a life full of woes.

Good and just I hear only jeers, oh!

Morning and night I suffer blows.

I make a belt of grasses' sweet, oh!

And add to it clovers and thymes.

My heart tells me it's good and meet, oh!

I won't regret to die nine times.

The Sacred One neglects his duty, oh!

He will not look into my heart.

The slanderers envy my beauty, oh!

They say I play licentious part.

The vulgar praise what is unfair, oh!

They reject common rules with pleasure.

They like the crooked and not the square, oh!

Accommodation is their measure.

Downcast, depressed and sad am I, oh!

Alone I bear sufferings long.

I would rather in exile die, oh!

Than mingle with the vulgar throng.

The eagle cleaves alone the air, oh!

Since olden days it has been fleet

The round cannot fit with the square, oh!

Who go different ways ne'er meet.

I curb my will and check my heart, oh!

Endure reproach as well as blame

I'd die to play a righteous part, oh!

The ancient sages would bear no shame.

Regretting I've gone a wrong way, oh!

I hesitate and will go back.

Before I go too far astray, oh!

I wheel my cab to former track.

I loose my horse by waterside, oh!

At Pepper Hill I take a rest.

I won't advance to turn the tide, oh!

I will retire to mend my vest.

I'll make a coat with lotus leaves, oh!

And patch my skirt with lilies white.

Unknown, I care not if it grieves, oh!

My heart will shed fragrance and light.

I raise my headdress towering high, oh!

And lengthen pendants sparkling long.

My fragrance 'mid the dirt won't die, oh!

My brilliancy ne'er wanes thereamong.

I look around and feast my sight, oh!

On scenes north and south, east and west.

My pendants seem all the more bright, oh!

My fragrance outshines all the rest.

All men delight in what they please, oh!

Alone I always love the beauty.

My body rent, my heart at ease, oh!

Can I change and neglect my duty?

这首诗感情充沛，简短有力。节选的这部分内容痛斥统治者的荒淫暴虐和大臣的追逐私利，陈述自己的政治主张，充分表达了诗人的忠君爱国思想；也让读者更加深刻地理解了诗人追求真理、宁死不屈的精神。这种精神集中体现了中华民族精神，给无数仁人志士以品行示范与精神动力。

The poem is emotional, brief and impactful. The excerpted part lambasted the ruler's extravagance and tyranny as well as the courtiers' pursuit of personal gain, stated the poet's political propositions, and fully expressed his loyal and patriotic thoughts, by which the reader can understand more deeply the unyielding spirit of the poet in his pursuit of truth that embodies the spirit of the Chinese nation and provides moral demonstration and spiritual motivation for countless people with lofty ideals.

涉江采芙蓉
Crossing the River to Pick Hibiscus

扫码看视频

《涉江采芙蓉》是《古诗十九首》中描写怀乡思亲的代表作，创作于东汉时期。两汉时期，经学成为士人跻身朝堂、谋求功名的重要资本，于是千千万万的学子离乡游学求宦京师。然而，如此众多的士人与官僚机构有限的职位，形成了一种得机幸进者少、失意向隅者多的局面，逐渐产生了一个坎壈失意的文人群体，即《古诗十九首》中的"游子"和"荡子"。这些失意的游子苦闷、忧伤，怀念故乡和亲人。

"Crossing the River to Pick Hibiscus" is a representative work in the collection *Nineteen Old Poems* that depicts homesickness and longing for family. It was created during the Eastern Han Dynasty. During the Western and Eastern Han periods, Confucian studies became an important capital for scholars to serve the country and seek official positions. As a result, countless scholars left their hometowns to study and pursue careers in the capital city.

However, with numerous scholars but limited positions in the bureaucratic system, only a few could succeed while many ended up being disappointed and marginalized. This gradually created a group of disheartened literati, known as "travelers" and "vagabonds" reflected in the collection *Nineteen Old Poems*. These frustrated travelers longed for their hometowns and loved ones, feeling dejected and sorrowful.

此诗借助他乡游子和家乡思妇采集芙蓉来表达相互之间的思念之情，深刻地反映了他们在现实生活与精神生活中的痛苦。全诗运用借景抒情及白描手法，从游子和思妇两个角度交错叙写，虚实结合，借思妇口吻悬想出游子"还顾望旧乡"的情景，把游子对故乡的望而难归之情抒写得极为凄婉，反映了一对同心离居夫妇的痛苦。

This poem expresses the mutual feelings of longing between a homesick traveler and a woman at home, using the collection of lotus flowers as a metaphor. It deeply reflects the agony they experience in both their physical and spiritual lives. The poem utilizes the techniques of expressing emotions through scenery and detailed description, alternately narrating from the perspectives of the traveler and the woman, and blending reality and imagination. Using the woman's voice, the poem imagines the scene of the traveler "looking back and gazing at his distant home", expressing the traveler's poignant longing for home in a heart-wrenching manner. This reflects the painful love between a couple who are separated but share the same feelings.

涉江采芙蓉

佚名

涉江采芙蓉，兰泽多芳草。

采之欲遗谁，所思在远道。

还顾望旧乡，长路漫浩浩。

同心而离居，忧伤以终老。

Crossing the River to Pick Hibiscus

Anonymity

Wading across the river for the lotus I go;

Over the marshes more fragrant flowers grow.

To whom do I want to send these blooms?

My thought follows the far-stretching road.

I look back and gaze at my distant home,

But the way looms as blurry as in a dream.

The two loving hearts are kept separated;

Sorrow will stay till my blood turns cold.

登 鹳 雀 楼
On the Stork Tower

扫码看视频

《登鹳雀楼》是唐代诗人王之涣的诗作。此诗前两句写的是自然景色，但开笔就有缩万里于咫尺，使咫尺有万里之势；后两句写意，写得出人意料，把哲理与景物、情势融合得天衣无缝。清代诗评家认为："王诗短短二十字，前十字大意已尽，后十字有尺幅千里之势。"此诗篇幅虽短，却绘下北国河山的磅礴气势和壮丽景象，气势磅礴、意境深远。特别是后两句，常常被引用，借以表达积极探索和无限进取的人生态度。

"On the Stork Tower" is a poem written by Wang Zhihuan, a poet in the Tang Dynasty. The first two lines of this poem are about natural scenery, yet create profound artistic conception from the beginning. The last two lines write about artistic conception in an unexpected manner, in which philosophy, scenery and situation dissolve seamlessly. Poetry critics in the Qing Dynasty thought, "Wang's poem has only 20 characters, the former ten characters of which convey the main idea and the latter ten words reflect profound artistic conception." Although short in length, the poem is a masterpiece which depicts the majestic momentum and magnificent scene of the rivers and mountains in northern China. Especially, the latter two lines are often quoted to express an actively exploratory and infinitely enterprising attitude towards life.

登鹳雀楼

王之涣

白日依山尽，黄河入海流。
欲穷千里目，更上一层楼。

On the Stork Tower

Wang Zhihuan

The sun along the mountain bows,

The Yellow River seawards flows.

You will enjoy a grander sight,

If you climb to a greater height.

　　前两句写所见，诗人遥望一轮落日向楼前一望无际、连绵起伏的群山西沉，在视野的尽头冉冉而下；目送流经楼前下方的黄河奔腾咆哮、滚滚南来，又在远处折而向东，流归大海。后两句写所想，写诗人一种无止境探求的愿望，还写想看得更远，看到目力所能达到的地方，唯一的办法就是要站得更高些。

　　The first two lines write about what the poet saw, when he looked at a setting sun sink into the endless and undulating mountains in front of the tower, and then slowly disappear at the end of his vision, and watched the Yellow River roaring beneath the tower, rolling from the south, turning east in the distance and flowing back to the sea. The last two lines write about the poet's desire to explore endlessly and enjoy a grander sight, the only way of which is to climb to a greater height.

　　诗人运用极其朴素、极其浅显的语言，把进入广阔视野的万里河山形象地收入诗中，这首诗描述了诗人在登高望远中表现出来的不凡的胸襟、抱负，反映了盛唐时期人们积极向上的进取精神。

　　The poet used extremely plain and simple words to vividly integrate vast rivers and mountains that entered the broad field of vision into the poem. This poem describes the poet's extraordinary ambition when he took a far-sighted view, reflecting the positive and enterprising spirit of people in the prosperous Tang Dynasty.

春　晓
Spring Morning

扫码看视频

　　《春晓》是唐代诗人孟浩然隐居在鹿门山时所作，诗人抓住在春天的早晨刚刚醒来时的一瞬间展开联想，描绘了一幅春天早晨绚丽的图景，生动地表达了诗人对春天的热爱和怜惜之情。

　　"Spring Morning" was written by Meng Haoran, a poet of the Tang Dynasty, when he lived in seclusion in Lumen Mountain. The poet captured the moment when he woke up on a spring morning and used it as a springboard for his imagination. He vividly portrayed a resplendent spring morning and articulated his profound love and pity for spring.

春　晓

孟浩然

春眠不觉晓，处处闻啼鸟。
夜来风雨声，花落知多少。

Spring Morning

Meng Haoran

This spring morning in bed I'm lying,

Not to awake till birds are crying.

After one night of wind and showers,

How many are the fallen flowers?

　　《春晓》的语言平易浅近，自然天成，一点也看不出人工雕琢的痕迹，而言浅意浓、景真情真，深得大自然的真趣。时间的跳跃、感情的微妙变化，都很富有情趣，能给人带来无

穷兴味。俗话说"一年之计在于春"，在我们每个人的意识里，春天代表了"新与生"，无论上一年过得如何，下一个春天的到来总是能再次赋予我们新的希望和迎接新的开始的勇气与动力，使我们脚踏实地地面对每一天。

The language of "Spring Morning" is simple, plain and natural, without any man-made polish. However, plain as the language is, the meaning is deep. With true scenery and emotions, it demonstrates the true interest of nature. The jump of time and the subtle changes of feelings are all very appealing and can bring endless interest to people. As the saying goes, "A year's plan starts with spring", which means that in everyone's mind, spring represents "new and alive". No matter how the previous year went, the arrival of the next spring can always give us new hope, courage and motivation to meet a new start, and live each day in a down-to-earth manner.

过 故 人 庄
Visiting an Old Friend's Cottage

扫码看视频

孟浩然是唐代著名的山水诗人，生于盛唐，早年有志用世，在仕途困顿、痛苦失望后，尚能自重，不媚俗世，修道归隐终生。

Meng Haoran was a famous landscape poet, born in the flourishing period of the Tang Dynasty. Ambitious in his early years, he was stranded in his official career and bitterly disappointed. Still self-dignified as he was, he did not ingratiate himself with the mundane world, and cloistered himself for life.

孟诗绝大部分为五言短篇，多写山水田园和隐居的逸兴以及羁旅行役的心情。其中既有愤世嫉俗之词，也有诗人对山水田园的称颂和向往。

Most of Meng's poems are short five-character poems, mainly about landscape, the freedom of living in seclusion, as well as the mood of traveling and staying in a strange place. There is cynicism, as well as praise and yearning for idyllic scenery in his poems.

过 故 人 庄

孟浩然

故人具鸡黍，邀我至田家。

绿树村边合，青山郭外斜。

开轩面场圃，把酒话桑麻。

待到重阳日，还来就菊花。

Visiting an Old Friend's Cottage

Meng Haoran

My friend's prepared chicken and rice;

I'm invited to his cottage hall.

Green trees surround the village nice;

Blue hills slant beyond city wall.

Windows open to field and ground;

Over wine we talk of crops of grain.

On Double Ninth Day I'll come around;

For the chrysanthemums again.

《过故人庄》是孟浩然早年隐居鹿门山时创作的。当时，孟浩然到山居朋友家做客，两人开怀畅饮、谈天说地，心情十分畅快。诗人沉醉于田园的雅静美丽和朋友的淳朴真挚之中，遂提笔写下了这首诗。此诗初看似乎平淡如水，但细细品味却犹如一幅描绘田园风光的中国画，将情与景完美地结合起来，具有很强的艺术感染力。诗由"邀"到"至"到"话"又到"还来"一径写去，自然流畅。语言朴实无华，意境清新隽永。诗人如话家常，其写田园景物清新雅静，写朋友情谊真挚深厚，写田家生活简朴悠然。

"Visiting an Old Friend's Cottage" was written when Meng Haoran lived in seclusion in Lumen Mountain in his early years. At that time, he paid a visit to an old friends's cottage, where they drank and talked freely and happily. Immersed in the tranquility and beauty of the countryside as well as the simpleness and sincerity of his friend, the poet wrote this poem. At first glance, it seems to be plain, and when tasted carefully, it is like a Chinese painting depicting pastoral scenery, which perfectly combines the scenes and has a strong artistic appeal. From "invitation" to "arrival" to "talk" and then to "coming around", the poem is written in a natural and smooth way. The language is simple and unadorned, while the artistic conception is fresh and meaningful. The poet writes the poem in a normal conversation way, where pastoral scenery is fresh and quiet, friendship is sincere and profound, and rural life is simple and leisurely.

送元二使安西
A Farewell Song

扫码看视频

《送元二使安西》是王维送朋友去西北边疆时所作的诗，作于安史之乱前，其送行之地是渭城。诗人送友人元二远赴安西都护府，从长安（今西安）一带送到渭城客舍，在分别之际作了这首七言绝句。此诗语言朴实，形象生动，运用了巧妙的艺术手法，表达了浓郁深挚的感情，道出了依依惜别之情。

"A Farewell Song" is a poem written by Wang Wei when he sent his friend to the northwest frontier. It was written before An-Shi Rebellion and the farewell place was Wei City. The poet escorted his friend Yuan Er to Anxi Frontier Command, from Chang'an (now Xi'an City) to the guest house of Wei City hotel, and on the occasion of farewell he made this seven-character quatrain. The poem is plain in language and vivid in image. Artfully using artistic techniques to express the strong and deep feelings, it reveals feelings of dependence and reluctance to bid farewell.

送元二使安西

王维

渭城朝雨浥轻尘，客舍青青柳色新。
劝君更尽一杯酒，西出阳关无故人。

A Farewell Song

Wang Wei

No dust is raised on the road wet with morning rain,

The willows by the hotel look so fresh and green.

I invite you to drink a cup of wine again,

West of the Sunny Pass no friends will be seen.

此诗前两句写渭城驿馆风景，交代送别的时间、地点、气候和环境；后两句转入伤别，却不着"伤"字，只用举杯劝酒来表达内心强烈深沉的惜别之情。全诗以明朗自然的语言抒发别情，写得情景交融、韵味深永，具有很强的艺术感染力，落成之后便被人配以管弦，广为传唱。这首诗所描写的是一种最具普遍性的离别，没有特殊的背景，蕴含深挚的惜别之情，适合绝大多数离别筵席演唱，后来编入乐府，并成为流传千古的名曲。

The first two lines of the poem describe the scenery of the guest house of Wei City, giving the time, place, weather and environment of farewell; the last two lines shift to the sorrowful farewell without sorrowful words, only expressing his strong and deep inner feelings of farewell by inviting his friend to drink. The whole poem expresses farewell feelings in clear and natural language, with the scenery depicted and the emotions expressed in perfect harmony, having a lasting and strong artistic appeal. After its completion, it is set to music and sung widely. This poem describes the most universal farewell with no special background, containing deep farewell feelings, suitable for most people to sing when bidding farewell. It was later compiled into the folk songs of Yuefu, and became a famous song down through the ages.

望庐山瀑布
The Waterfall in Mount Lu Viewed from Afar

扫码看视频

《望庐山瀑布》是唐诗代表作。唐玄宗开元十三年（公元725 年），李白出游金陵（今南京）途中初游庐山，偶遇瀑布美景，震撼之下作下此诗。

"The Waterfall in Mount Lu Viewed from Afar" is a famous representative poem of the Tang Dynasty. In the 13th year of Kaiyuan under the reign of Emperor Xuanzong of the Tang Dynasty (725 CE), Li Bai first visited Mount Lu on his way to Jinling (the ancient name of Nanjing). He was struck by the beauty of the waterfall and wrote this poem.

望庐山瀑布

李白

日照香炉生紫烟，

遥看瀑布挂前川。

飞流直下三千尺，

疑是银河落九天。

The Waterfall in Mount Lu Viewed from Afar

Li Bai

The sunlit Censer Peak exhales incense-like cloud,

Like an upended stream the cataract sounds loud.

Its torrent dashes down three thousand feet from high

As if the Silver River[1] fell from the blue sky.

李白被后人誉为"诗仙"，是一位伟大的浪漫主义诗人，《望庐山瀑布》虽只有寥寥四句，却充分体现了李白的浪漫和洒脱。山顶紫烟缭绕，山间白练悬挂，山下激流奔腾，构成一幅绚丽壮美的图景。巍巍香炉峰藏在云烟雾霭之中，从远处遥望，瀑布似乎从云端飞流直下，凌空而落，如同一条银河。李白的浪漫洒脱为后人传颂。

Li Bai is praised as "the Immortal Poet" by later generations, is a great romantic poet. Although there are only four lines in this poem, it fully reflects Li Bai's romance and unrestrained spirit. Incense-like cloud wreathes the top of the mountain, the waterfall upends along the mountain and the torrent of the waterfall dashes at the foot of the mountain, all of which constitute a gorgeous and magnificent picture. The Censer Peak is hidden in the clouds and mists. Looking at the waterfall from afar, it is like the Silver River flowing straight down from the clouds. Therefore, the romance, and free and easy nature of Li Bai were passed down and praised by later generations.

1　The Chinese name for the Milky Way.

行路难（其一）

Hard Is the Way of the World (One)

扫码看视频

天宝元年（公元 742 年），李白奉召入京，出任翰林供奉，傲气、才气并存的李白自然不可能与官场的世俗同流合污，因此惨遭权臣排挤，两年后被"赐金放还"，被变相地撵出了长安。盛唐之下无容身之所，"诗仙"李白怀着对仕路艰难的愤慨写下了这首诗。

In the first year of Tianbao (742 CE), Li Bai was summoned to the capital and served in the Imperial Academy. Li Bai, both proud and talented, naturally could not be in league with the secular officialdom, and was excluded by powerful ministers. Two years later, he was "awarded money and released", and driven out of Chang'an in a disguised form. There was no place to stay under the prosperous Tang Dynasty, so Li Bai, "the Immortal Poet", wrote this poem with his indignation at the difficulty of his career.

行路难（其一）

李白

金樽清酒斗十千，玉盘珍羞直万钱。

停杯投箸不能食，拔剑四顾心茫然。

欲渡黄河冰塞川，将登太行雪满山。

闲来垂钓碧溪上，忽复乘舟梦日边。

行路难，行路难，多歧路，今安在？

长风破浪会有时，直挂云帆济沧海。

Hard Is the Way of the World (One)

Li Bai

Pure wine in golden cup costs ten thousand coppers, good!

Choice dish in a jade plate is worth as much, nice food!

Pushing aside my cup and chopsticks, I can't eat;

Drawing my sword and looking round, I hear my heart beat.

I can't cross Yellow River: Ice has stopped its flow;

I can't climb Mount Taihang: The sky is blind with snow.

I poise a fishing pole with ease on the green stream,

Or set sail for the sun like the sage in a dream.

Hard is the way, hard is the way.

Don't go astray! Whither today?

A time will come to ride the wind and cleave the waves;

I'll set my cloudlike sail to cross the sea which raves.

　　《行路难（其一）》是李白作的一首七言古诗，开篇描写丰盛隆重的宴会场面，亦是感谢友人盛情款待他这即将漂泊之人。诗人用"心茫然""冰塞川""雪满山"，感叹"行路难"，伟大的政治抱负成为泡影，空怀一颗报国之心却落得"赐金放还"的地步。但李白拥有绝不会被落寞仕途击垮的浪漫仙人的强大内心。尽管黑暗政治带来了苦闷、愤郁和不平，但他想到姜尚、伊尹时，境界顿开。这首诗表现了诗人的倔强、自信和他对理想的执着追求，他把乐观种植在苦难之上，重树信心与豪情，"长风破浪会有时，直挂云帆济沧海"。

　　"Hard Is the Way of the World (One)" is an ancient seven-character poem written by Li Bai, which begins with the description of a sumptuous banquet scene and expresses the poet's gratitude to his friends for their hospitality to him who was about to live in a strange land and lead a wandering life. The poet used "hear my heart beat", "Ice has stopped its flow" and "The sky is blind with snow" to lament that "Hard is the way", for his great political ambitions had come to naught and the hope of serving the country ended up with being "awarded money and released". But Li Bai had a strong heart of a romantic immortal who would never be defeated by the disappointed career, although the dark politics brought bitterness, anger and injustice. When he thought of Jiang Shang and Yi Yin, his mindset became more open. The poem shows the poet's stubbornness, self-confidence and his persistent pursuit of the ideal. Planting optimism on the suffering and re-treeing confidence and heroic feelings, he believed that "A time will come to ride the wind and cleave the waves; I'll set my cloudlike sail to cross the sea which raves."

全诗立足李白的仕途坎坷和渺茫的政治前途，却以独到的浪漫主义手法和角度唱出了高昂乐观的调子，流传后世，成为后人勉励自己的绝代佳句。

The whole poem is based on Li Bai's bumpy official career, and bleak political prospects, but it sings in a high-spirited and optimistic tone with the poet's unique romantic techniques and angles, which is passed down by the later generations and becomes an excellent quote for the later generations to encourage themselves.

蜀 道 难
Hard Is the Road to Shu

扫码看视频

　　《蜀道难》是李白的代表作之一。诗人用乐府古题，以浪漫主义的手法展开丰富的想象，以蜀道奇丽磅礴展现山川之壮美，以蜀道高危难行寓意仕途之坎坷，反映了诗人在长期漂泊中怀才不遇的愤懑之情。

　　The poem "Hard Is the Road to Shu" is one of Li Bai's representative works. By the old title of Yuefu poetry, the poet uses his imagination in a romantic way, shows the magnificent beauty of mountains and rivers by depicting the splendors of the road to Shu, and conveys the ups and downs of his official career with the high danger of the road, reflecting his embitterment for talent remained unrecognized in his wanderings.

蜀 道 难

李白

噫吁嚱，危乎高哉！

蜀道之难，难于上青天！

蚕丛及鱼凫，开国何茫然！

尔来四万八千岁，不与秦塞通人烟。

西当太白有鸟道，可以横绝峨眉巅。

地崩山摧壮士死，然后天梯石栈相钩连。

上有六龙回日之高标，下有冲波逆折之回川。

黄鹤之飞尚不得过，猿猱欲度愁攀援。

青泥何盘盘，百步九折萦岩峦。

扪参历井仰胁息，以手抚膺坐长叹。

问君西游何时还？畏途巉岩不可攀。

但见悲鸟号古木，雄飞雌从绕林间。

又闻子规啼夜月，愁空山。

蜀道之难，难于上青天，使人听此凋朱颜！

连峰去天不盈尺，枯松倒挂倚绝壁。

飞湍瀑流争喧豗，砯崖转石万壑雷。

其险也如此，嗟尔远道之人胡为乎来哉！

剑阁峥嵘而崔嵬，一夫当关，万夫莫开。

所守或匪亲，化为狼与豺。

朝避猛虎，夕避长蛇，磨牙吮血，杀人如麻。

锦城虽云乐，不如早还家。

蜀道之难，难于上青天，侧身西望长咨嗟！

Hard Is the Road to Shu

Li Bai

Oho! Behold! How steep! How high!

The road to Shu is harder than to climb the sky.

Since the two pioneers

Put the kingdom in order,

Have passed forty-eight thousand years,

And few have tried to pass its border.

There's a bird track o'er Great White Mountain to the west,

Which cut through Mountain Eyebrows by the crest.

The crust crumbled, five serpent-killing heroes slain,

Along the cliffs a rocky path was hacked then.

Above stand peaks too high for the sun to pass o'er.

Below the torrents run back and forth, churn and roar.

Even the Golden Crane can't fly across;

How to climb over, gibbons are at a loss.

What tortuous mountain path Green Mud Ridge faces!

Around the top we turn nine turns each hundred paces.

Looking up breathless, I can touch the stars nearby,

Beating my breast, I sink aground with long, long sigh.

When will you come back from this journey to the west?

How can you climb up dangerous path and mountain crest?

Where can you hear on ancient trees but sad birds wail

And see the female birds fly, followed by the male?

And hear home-going cuckoos weep

Beneath the moon in mountains deep?

The road to Shu is harder than to climb the sky,

On hearing this, your cheeks would lose their rosy dye.

Between the sky and peaks there is not a foot's space,

And ancient pines hang, head down, from the cliff's surface.

And cataracts and torrents, dash on boulders under,

Roaring like thousands of echoes of thunder.

So dangerous these places are,

Alas! Why should you come here from afar?

Rugged is a path between the cliffs, steep and high,

Guarded by one. And forced by none.

Disloyal guards

Would turn wolves and pards,

Man-eating tigers at daybreak.

And at dusk, blood-sucking long snake.

One may make merry in the Town of Silk, I know,

But I would rather homeward go.

The road to Shu is harder than to climb to the sky,

I'd turn and westward look with long, long sigh.

全诗二百九十四个字，以天马行空的想象，用荡气回肠的文字，描摹蜀道上的陡峭艰险，表达了诗人对追求理想道路上的艰难之叹，同时隐隐流露出诗人对国事的忧虑与关切。用山川之险言蜀道之难，给人以回肠荡气之感，充分体现了诗人的浪漫气质和热爱祖国的感情。

The 294-character poem, which depicts the steep and hard road to Shu with wild imagination and touching words, expresses the poet's lament about the difficulty in pursuing his ideals as well as reveales his concerns for the country. By depicting the dangerous mountains and rivers along the hard road to Shu, the poem gives people a soul-stirring feeling, fully demonstrating the poet's romantic temperament and love for his motherland.

早发白帝城
Leaving the White Emperor Town at Dawn

扫码看视频

　　唐肃宗乾元二年（公元 759 年）春天，李白因永王李璘案被流放夜郎（今贵州桐梓一带），取道四川赶赴被贬谪的地方。行至白帝城的时候，忽然收到自己被赦免的消息，李白惊喜万分，随即乘舟东下江陵。此诗即回舟抵江陵时所作。

　　In the spring of the second year of Qianyuan (759 CE) of Emperor Suzong of Tang, Li Bai was exiled to Yelang (now Tongzi area, Guizhou Province) because of the case of Li Lin, the Prince Yong, and went to the place where he was exiled by way of Sichuan. When he arrived at the White Emperor Town, he suddenly received the news that he was amnestied. He was so pleasantly surprised that he went east to Jiangling by boat. This poem was written when he arrived at Jiangling in a return boat.

早发白帝城
李白

朝辞白帝彩云间，

千里江陵一日还。

两岸猿声啼不住，

轻舟已过万重山。

Leaving the White Emperor Town at Dawn
Li Bai

Leaving at dawn the White Emperor crowned with cloud,

I've sailed a thousand miles through canyons in a day.

With monkeys' sad adieus the riverbanks are loud;

My skiff has left ten thousand mountains far away.

　　《早发白帝城》是李白诗作中流传最为广泛的名篇之一，全诗洋溢着诗人经历艰难岁月之后重新焕发出的激情。诗人把轻快的心情和长江两岸山川秀美景色融为一体，

在雄峻和迅疾中有豪情和欢悦，快船快意给读者留下了广阔的想象空间。这首诗风格飘逸流畅，意境悠远，读起来就能感受到诗人的轻快与愉悦。

"Leaving the White Emperor Town at Dawn" is one of the most popular masterpieces of Li Bai, and the whole poem is full of the poet's passion after he went through a difficult time. The poet blends a cheerful mood with the beautiful scenery of the mountains and rivers on both sides of the Yangtze River, exuding lofty sentiments and joy amidst majesty and speed, which leave readers with vast space for imagination. This poem is elegant and fluent in style, with profound artistic conception. Reading it, we can feel the poet's lightness and joy.

别 董 大

Farewell to Dong Da

扫码看视频

唐玄宗天宝六载（公元 747 年）春天，吏部尚书房琯被贬出朝廷，其门客董庭兰也离开长安，而这年冬天，高适与董庭兰会于睢阳（故址在今河南省商丘市南），高适遂写下了《别董大》。

In the spring of 747 CE, the sixth year of Tianbao (the reign title of Emperor Xuanzong of the Tang Dynasty), Fang Guan, the Minister of Personnel, was demoted from the court, and his follower Dong Tinglan also left Chang' an. In the winter of the same year, Gao Shi and Dong Tinglan met in Suiyang (formerly located in the south of present-day Shangqiu City, Henan Province) and the former wrote "Farewell to Dong Da".

别 董 大

高适

千里黄云白日曛，

北风吹雁雪纷纷。

莫愁前路无知己，

天下谁人不识君。

Farewell to Dong Da

Gao Shi

Yellow clouds spread for miles and miles have veiled the day,

The north wind blows down snow and wild geese fly away.

Fear not you've no admirers as you go along,

There is no connoisseur on earth but loves your song.

《别董大》是唐代诗人高适创作的一首送别诗。诗的前两句写景，从中可见诗人内心之忧郁。虽不涉人和事，却已使人如置身风雪之中，似闻山巅水涯有壮士长啸。

以内心之真，写别离愁绪，故能深挚；以胸襟之宽，叙眼前景色，故能悲壮。后两句言辞婉转劝慰友人，于慰藉中充满着信心和力量，激励朋友抖擞精神去奋斗、去拼搏，足见诗人豪迈豁达的胸襟及其与友人的深厚情谊。

"Farewell to Dong Da" is a farewell poem written by Gao Shi, a poet of the Tang Dynasty. The first two lines depict the scenery to reveal the inner depression. Though no people and things involved, it has made people feel like being in the midst of wind and snow, hearing a heroic man roaring on the cliff of the mountain. True to the heart, one can write about the sadness of farewell so sincerely; with open-mindedness, one can describe the scenery so solemnly and stirringly. The last two lines console his friend with tactful words, which are full of confidence and strength, inspiring him to struggle and work hard, demonstrating the poet's boldness and open-mindedness as well as their deep friendship.

这首诗之所以卓绝，是因为高适"多胸臆语，兼有气骨"（殷璠《河岳英灵集》）、"以气质自高"（《唐诗纪事》），因而能为志士增色，为游子拭泪。

The reason why this poem is so outstanding is that Gao Shi "conveys his innermost feelings in a free and unrestrained manner, and his poem has a natural character" (Yin Fan's *A Collection of the Poems in the Heyday of the Tang Dynasty*), and "with strength of character" (*The Chronicle of Tang Poetry*), which can give a boost to people with lofty ideals and wipe tears for wanderers.

白雪歌送武判官归京
Song of White Snow in Farewell to Secretary Wu Going Back to the Capital

扫码看视频

这是岑参边塞诗的代表作，是一篇入情入景的送别诗，作于他第二次出塞时期。此时，他很受安西节度使封常青的器重，他的大多数边塞诗都成于这一时期。在这首诗中，诗人以细腻的笔触描绘了冬天银装素裹的盛况，通过细节描写表达他对武判官的依依不舍之情，表现了他们深厚亲密的友情，展现了唐代诗人的文学魅力。

This is the representative work of Cen Shen's frontier fortress poems, a touching farewell poem composed during his second expedition. At that time, he was highly appreciated by Feng Changqing, the governor of Anxi, and most of his frontier fortress poems were written in this period. In this poem, the poet depicts the majestic winter scenery with delicate strokes, and expresses his reluctance to part from secretary Wu through detailed descriptions, showing their profound and intimate friendship, revealing the literary charm of Tang Dynasty poets.

白雪歌送武判官归京

岑参

北风卷地白草折，胡天八月即飞雪。

忽如一夜春风来，千树万树梨花开。

散入珠帘湿罗幕，狐裘不暖锦衾薄。

将军角弓不得控，都护铁衣冷难着。

瀚海阑干百丈冰，愁云惨淡万里凝。

中军置酒饮归客，胡琴琵琶与羌笛。

纷纷暮雪下辕门，风掣红旗冻不翻。

轮台东门送君去，去时雪满天山路。

山回路转不见君，雪上空留马行处。

Song of White Snow in Farewell to Secretary Wu Going Back to the Capital
Cen Shen

Snapping the pallid grass, the northern wind whirls low;

In the eighth moon the Tartar sky is filled with snow.

As if the vernal breeze had come back overnight,

Adorning thousands of pear trees with blossoms white.

Flakes enter pearled blinds and wet the silken screen;

No furs of fox can warm us nor brocade quilts green.

The general cannot draw his rigid bow with ease;

E'en the commissioner in coat of mail would freeze.

A thousand feet o'er cracked wilderness ice piles,

And gloomy clouds hang sad and drear for miles and miles.

We drink in headquarters to our guest homeward bound;

With Tartar lutes, pipas and pipes the camps resound.

Snow in large flakes at dusk falls heavy on camp gate;

The frozen red flag in the wind won't undulate.

At eastern gate of Wheel Tower we bid goodbye

On the snow-covered road to Heaven's Mountain high.

I watch his horse go past a bend and, lost to sight,

His track will soon be buried up by snow in flight.

　　这首诗以奇丽多变的雪景、开合自如的结构、抑扬顿挫的韵律，准确、鲜明、生动地描绘出奇中有丽、丽中有奇的美好意境，展现了唯美和浪漫的一面。同时，全诗不断变换着白雪画面，化景为情，慷慨悲壮，浑然雄劲，抒发了诗人对友人的依依惜别之情和因友人返京而产生的惆怅之情。这种景象与情感的融合给读者留下了深刻的印象，是一首不可多得的边塞佳作。

　　This poem, with its magnificent and varied snow sceneries, a freely openable structure, and the cadenced rhythm, accurately and vividly creates a wonderful artistic conception that is surprisingly beautiful and romantic. At the same time, the whole poem constantly changes snow sceneries and translates them into emotions, fervently, solemnly and stirringly as well as vigorously, expressing the poet's reluctant farewell to his friend and the feeling of melancholy caused by his friend's going back to the capital. The integration of sceneries and emotions in this poem leaves a deep impression on the reader, which makes it a rare masterpiece of frontier fortress poems.

兵 车 行
Song of Conscripts

扫码看视频

《兵车行》是唐代诗人杜甫创作的叙事诗。关于该诗的创作背景有两种观点，一种观点认为该诗是因唐玄宗用兵吐蕃而作，另一种观点认为该诗是因唐玄宗在天宝十载（公元751年）出兵南诏而作。诗人运用乐府民歌的形式，深刻地反映了频繁的战争给人民带来的巨大灾难。

"Song of the Conscripts" is a narrative poem written by Du Fu in the Tang Dynasty. There are two viewpoints on the background of the creation of this poem. One is that it was written because Emperor Xuanzong of Tang Dynasty led troops to fight against Tubo, while the other believes it was written because Emperor Xuanzong led a military campaign against the kingdom of Nanzhao in the tenth year of the Tianbao period (751 CE). The poet used the form of Yuefu folk songs to profoundly reflect the great disasters caused by frequent wars to the people.

兵 车 行
杜甫

车辚辚，马萧萧，行人弓箭各在腰。

耶娘妻子走相送，尘埃不见咸阳桥。

牵衣顿足拦道哭，哭声直上干云霄。

道旁过者问行人，行人但云点行频。

或从十五北防河，便至四十西营田。

去时里正与裹头，归来头白还戍边。

边庭流血成海水，武皇开边意未已。

君不闻汉家山东二百州，千村万落生荆杞。

纵有健妇把锄犁，禾生陇亩无东西。

况复秦兵耐苦战，被驱不异犬与鸡。

长者虽有问，役夫敢申恨？

且如今年冬，未休关西卒。

县官急索租，租税从何出？

信知生男恶，反是生女好。

生女犹得嫁比邻，生男埋没随百草。

君不见，青海头，古来白骨无人收。

新鬼烦冤旧鬼哭，天阴雨湿声啾啾！

Song of the Conscripts
Du Fu

Chariots rumble

And horses grumble.

The conscripts march with bow and arrows at the waist.

Their fathers, mothers, wives and children come in haste to see them off;

The bridge is shrouded in dust they've raised.

They clutch at their coats, stamp the feet and bar the way;

Their grief cries loud and strikes the cloud straight, straight away.

An onlooker by roadside asks an enrollee.

"The conscription is frequent," only answers he.

Some went north at fifteen to guard the rivershore,

And were sent west to till the land at forty or more.

The elder bound their young heads when they went away;

Just home, they're sent to the frontier though their hair's gray.

The field on borderland becomes a sea of blood;

The emperor's greed for land is still at high flood.

Have you not heard

Two hundred districts east of the Hua Mountains lie,

Where briers and brambles grow in villages far and nigh?

Although stout women can wield the plough and the hoe,

Thorns and weeds in the east as in the west o'ergrow

The enemy are used to hard and stubborn fight;

Our men are driven just like dogs or fowls in flight.

You are kind to ask me

To complain I'm not free.

In winter of this year

Conscription goes on here.

The magistrates for taxes press.

How can we pay them in distress?

If we had known sons bring no joy,

We would have preferred girl to boy.

A daughter can be wed to a neighbor, alas!

A son can only be buried under the grass!

Have you not seen on borders green

Bleached bones since olden days unburied on the plain?

The old ghosts weep and cry, while the new ghosts complain;

The air is loud with screech and scream in gloomy rain.

　　诗歌开篇摹写送别的惨状，是纪事。诗人从蓦然而起的客观描述开始，以重墨铺染的雄浑笔法，如风至潮来，突兀展现出一幅震人心弦的巨幅送别图：车马人流，灰尘弥漫；哭声遍野，直冲云天。本诗从听觉和视觉上表现生死离别的悲惨场面，集中展现了成千上万个家庭妻离子散的悲剧。

　　The poem begins with a description of a heart-wrenching farewell, unveiling a vivid picture. Starting from an objective description of the sudden event, the poet used a powerful brushstroke, like blowing gust or rushing tides, to present a thrilling and heart-rending farewell picture: horse-drawn vehicles, crowds of people, and dust-filled surroundings; cries of despair echoing throughout the land and reaching the sky. Through the portrayal of the tragic scene of parting that is not easy to see each other again from both an auditory and visual perspective, the poem concentrates on the tragedy of thousands of families torn apart.

自"道旁过者问行人"始，传达征夫的诉苦，是纪言。诗人以设问方式，让征夫直接控诉战争给百姓带来的灾难。"点行频"一针见血地点出了造成百姓妻离子散、万民无辜牺牲、全国田亩荒芜的根源。最后把矛头直接指向了最高统治者唐玄宗，充分表达了诗人的悲愤之情。

From the line "An onlooker by roadside asks an enrollee" onwards, the poem conveys the grievances of the conscripts, offering a heartbreaking account. Through the use of questioning, the poem allows the conscripts to directly accuse the calamities brought about by the war to the people. The line "The conscription is frequent", directly points out the root causes of family separation, the innocent sacrifice of the people, and the devastation of the nation's fields. Finally, the poem directly targets the supreme ruler Emperor Xuanzong of the Tang Dynasty, fully expressing the poet's uncontrollable anger and indignation.

从"长者虽有问"到结尾"声啾啾"，诗人再次以问答方式揭露战争带来的灾难。通过当事人的口述，从抓兵、逼租两方面揭露了统治者的穷兵黩武给人民带来的双重灾难。接着，诗人以无比愤慨的笔调写出生男不如生女好，并以哀痛的笔调描绘了青海湖边古战场阴森寂冷的情景，令人不寒而栗，这都是统治者"开边意未已"造成的恶果。

From "You are kind to ask me" to "The air is loud with screech and scream" at the end, the poet once again reveals disasters brought about by the war through the use of a question-and-answer format. Through the narration of the people involved, the poet reveals the dual calamities caused by the belligerent rulers' capturing men as soldiers and pressing for land rent and imposing heavy taxes. Then, the poet wrote in an indignant tone that is was better to have daughters than sons, and described the gloomy and cold scene of an ancient battlefield by the Qinghai Lake in a mournful tone, which was chilling. All of these are the evil consequences caused by the fact that "the emperor's greed for land is still at high flood".

全诗寓情于叙事之中，在叙述次序上参差错落、前后呼应，变化开合井然有序，并巧妙运用过渡句和习用词语，产生了回肠荡气的艺术效果。

The poem weaves emotions into the narrative, with a narrative sequence that is deliberately staggered and interlinked, creating a well-organized structure of change and unity. It skillfully employs transitional sentences and familiar phrases, producing an artistic effect that stirs the heart and captivates the soul.

春 夜 喜 雨

Happy Rain on a Spring Night

扫码看视频

　　纵赏诗歌，"春雨"汇聚浩如烟海，而在所有描写春雨的唐诗里，杜甫可谓留下了浓墨重彩的一笔。《春夜喜雨》写于唐肃宗上元二年（公元 761 年）春天，此时杜甫因陕西旱灾来到四川成都，在草堂居住。他亲自耕作，种菜养花，与农民交往，对"贵如油"的春雨情深意切，因而写下了这首描写春夜降雨润泽万物的千古名篇。

　　Take a broader look at the poetry, there is a tremendous amount of spring rain-related poems, and in all Tang poems describing spring rain, Du Fu can be said to have left an indelible mark. "Happy Rain on a Spring Night" was written in the spring of 761 CE, the second year of Shangyuan (the reign title of Emperor Suzong of the Tang Dynasty), when Du Fu came to Chengdu, Sichuan Province due to a drought in Shaanxi and then lived in a cottage. He himself farmed, grew vegetables and flowers, interacted with peasants, and had a deep affection for spring rain which was "precious as oil", so he wrote this immortal poem which describes the rain on a spring night moistening every thing.

春 夜 喜 雨

杜甫

好雨知时节，当春乃发生。

随风潜入夜，润物细无声。

野径云俱黑，江船火独明。

晓看红湿处，花重锦官城。

Happy Rain on a Spring Night

Du Fu

Good rain knows its time right; It will fall when comes spring.

With wind it steals in night; Mute, it moistens each thing.

Over wild lanes dark cloud spreads; In boat a lantern looms.

Dawn sees saturated reds; The town's heavy with blooms.

　　《春夜喜雨》是唐代诗人杜甫创作的一首五言律诗，是一篇描绘春夜雨景、表现诗人喜悦心情的名作。一个"好"字开篇，再妙用拟人手法，将春雨描绘得善解人意、知晓时节——在万物萌芽生长的季节、人们需要的时候悄然而至。诗人用一系列的动词生动形象地描绘出春雨润泽万物的场景，再用情景交融的手法描写春雨到来之后的景色，侧面体现出作者对春雨的喜爱之切、对春景的喜悦之深，可谓一切景语皆情语。浦起龙说："写雨切夜易，切春难。"这首诗不仅切夜、切春，而且写出了春雨无私奉献的高尚品格，表现了诗人内敛而不张扬、奉献而不求回报的高尚品格。

"Happy Rain on a Spring Night" is an eight-line poem with five characters in a line, written by the Tang Dynasty poet Du Fu. It is a masterpiece which depicts the rain on a spring night and expresses a joyful mood. Starting with the word "good", it makes ingenious use of personification to depict spring rain as understanding as if "it knows its time right" and "steals in" when all things sprout and grow and people need it. The poet uses a series of verbs to vividly depict the scene of the spring rain moistening every thing, and then, by a fusion of feelings with scenes, describes the scenery after its arrival, reflecting indirectly his deep affection for the spring rain and great delight for the spring scenery. It may be said that all scenes are feelings. According to Pu Qilong, "It is easy to associate rain with night, but not spring." This poem not only involves night and spring, but also shows the noble character of selfless dedication of spring rain as well as the noble personality of the poet, who is reserved and unassuming, and dedicated without expecting anything in return.

江南逢李龟年

Coming across a Disfavored Court Musician on the Southern Shore of the Yangtze River

扫码看视频

杜甫少年时才华卓著，常出入于岐王李隆范和中书监崔涤的门庭，得以欣赏宫廷歌唱家李龟年的歌唱艺术。安史之乱后，杜甫漂泊到江南一带。大历四年（公元 769 年）三月，杜甫离开岳阳到潭州（在今湖南长沙），居留到第二年春天，和流落江南潭州的李龟年重逢。杜甫回忆起在友人府邸与李龟年频繁相见和听他唱歌的情景，感慨万千，于是写下这首诗。

Brilliant in his youth, Du Fu was a frequent visitor to the courtyards of Li Longfan, the Lord of Qi, and Cui Di, the secretariat supervisor (zhongshujian), where he was enabled to appreciate the singing art of the court musician Li Guinian. After the An-Shi Rebellion, Du Fu drifted to the regions south of the Yangtze River. In March of the fourth year of the Dali era (769 CE), Du Fu left Yueyang for Tanzhou (in today's Changsha, Hunan Province) and stayed there until the following spring. It was in Tanzhou that he met Li Guinian, who had been wandering there. Du Fu recalled the frequent meeting and listening to music at his friends' courtyards, and was filled with all sorts of emotions, so he wrote this poem.

江南逢李龟年

杜甫

岐王宅里寻常见，
崔九堂前几度闻。
正是江南好风景，
落花时节又逢君。

Coming across a Disfavored Court Musician on the Southern Shore of the Yangtze River

Du Fu

How oft in princely mansions did we meet,

As oft in lordly halls I heard you sing.

Now the southern scenery is most sweet,

But I meet you again in parting spring.

诗中没有正面描述时事，但通过一个人的命运和诗人的追忆感喟，展现了安史之乱给人们造成的巨大灾难和带来的心灵创伤。此诗抚今思昔，感慨万千。前两句是追忆昔日与李龟年的接触，寄寓着诗人对开元盛世的缅怀之情；后两句是对安史之乱后国事凋零、艺人颠沛流离的感慨。全诗语言极平易，而寓意极深远，内涵极丰满，世境离乱、年华盛衰、人情聚散，都浓缩在这短短的二十八字之中。

There is no direct description of current events in the poem, but through one's fate and the poet's recollection and lamentation, it shows the great disaster and psychological trauma caused by the An-Shi Rebellion. This poem recalls the past in the light of the present, with countless emotions. The first two lines are the poet's recollection of the contact with Li Guinian in the past, conveying his nostalgia for the

flourishing Kaiyuan Reign Period; the last two lines are his lamentation about the declined state affairs and the displaced artists after the An-Shi Rebellion. The language of the poem is plain, but the meaning is extremely profound and the connotation is extremely rich. The chaotic world, the vicissitudes of life, and the separation and reunion of human relationship are all condensed in just these twenty-eight characters.

丽 人 行
Satire on Fair Ladies

扫码看视频

　　唐朝是中国历史上非常繁荣和强盛的时期，但自武后以来，外戚擅权已成为唐朝统治阶层中一种普遍存在的现象。这些外戚利用自己的权力和地位大肆掠夺民脂民膏，引起了广大人民的强烈不满，这也是后来酿成安史之乱的主要原因之一。

　　The Tang Dynasty was a very prosperous and powerful period in Chinese history, but since Empress Wu's reign, relatives controlling power has become a common phenomenon in the ruling class then. They leveraged their power and status to plunder the wealth of the nation and its people, which aroused strong dissatisfaction of the people and turned out to be one of the primary causes for the An-Shi Rebellion later.

　　《丽人行》是一首采用乐府民歌形式反映现实生活的诗，通过描写杨氏兄妹曲江春游的情景，反映了君王的昏庸和时政的腐朽，以及安史之乱前夕的社会现实。

　　"Satire on Fair Ladies" is a Yuefu poem reflecting the real life in the form of Yuefu folk songs. By describing the scene of Yang Yuhuan's spring outing with her siblings along the Qujiang River, it reflects the incompetence of the ruler and the decadence of the government, as well as the social reality on the eve of the An-Shi Rebellion.

丽 人 行
杜甫

三月三日天气新，长安水边多丽人。

态浓意远淑且真，肌理细腻骨肉匀。

绣罗衣裳照暮春，蹙金孔雀银麒麟。

头上何所有？翠微匎叶垂鬓唇。

背后何所见？珠压腰衱稳称身。

就中云幕椒房亲，赐名大国虢与秦。

紫驼之峰出翠釜，水精之盘行素鳞。

犀箸厌饫久未下，鸾刀缕切空纷纶。

黄门飞鞚不动尘，御厨络绎送八珍。

萧鼓哀吟感鬼神，宾从杂遝实要津。

后来鞍马何逡巡，当轩下马入锦茵。

杨花雪落覆白苹，青鸟飞去衔红巾。

炙手可热势绝伦，慎莫近前丞相嗔！

Satire on Fair Ladies

Du Fu

The weather's fine in the third moon[1] on the third day. By riverside so many beauties in array.

Each of the ladies has a fascinating face. Their skin is delicate, their manners full of grace.

Embroidered with peacocks and unicorns in gold. Their dress in rich silks shines so bright when spring is old.

What do they wear on the head? Emerald pendant leaves hang down in silver thread.

What do you see from behind? How nice-fitting are their waist bands with pearls combined.

Among them there're the emperor's favorite kin. Ennobled Duchess of Guo comes with Duchess of Qin.

What do they eat? The purple meat

Of camel's hump cooked in green cauldron as a dish; On crystal plate is served snow-white slices of raw fish.

See rhino chopsticks the satiated eaters stay. And untouched morsels carved by belled knives on the tray.

When eunuchs' horses come running, no dust is raised; They bring still more rare dishes delicious to the taste.

Listen to soul-stirring music of flutes and drums! On the main road an official retinue comes.

A rider ambles on saddled horse, the last of all. He alights, treads on satin carpet, enters the hall.

The willow down-like snow falls on the duckweed white; The blue bird picking red handkerchief goes in flight.

The prime minister's powerful without a peer. His angry touch would bum your hand. Do not come near!

---

1 month.

　　此诗开篇着重描写众多丽人曲江春游的热闹场景和体貌、服饰，先泛写游春丽人的娴雅意态、优美体态和华丽衣着，引出主角杨氏姐妹的娇艳姿色。紧接着转入宴饮描写，以器皿雅致、肴馔精美、声乐动听烘托出杨氏兄妹的显赫与盛宠。最后写杨国忠的鞍马之势和入宴之态，并借用典故刻画出其声势烜赫和骄横跋扈。通篇只是写"丽人"们的生活情形，却达到了如前人所说"无一刺讥语，描摹处语语刺讥"的艺术效果。

　　This poem begins with a focus on the lively scene, physical appearance and clothes of many beauties who went for a spring outing along the Qujiang River. It first writes about the graceful manner, elegant figure and gorgeous clothes of the ladies generally, leading to the delicate beauty of the protagonists, the Yang sisters. Then it shifts to the description of the banquet with elegant vessels, fine food and beautiful music, setting off the prominence and glory of the Yang sisters. Finally, it writes about how Yang Guozhong (a cousin of the Yang sisters and also a senior official) ambles on saddled horse and enters the hall, depicting his great influence and arrogance by allusions. Though the whole poem just depicts the life situation of the "fair women", but it has achieved the artistic effect of "being satirical in each depiction though no satirical words are used" as said by predecessors.

枫桥夜泊
Mooring by Maple Bridge at Night

扫码看视频

《枫桥夜泊》是唐朝诗人张继的诗作。安史之乱爆发后，次年六月唐玄宗仓皇奔蜀。因为当时江南政局比较安定，所以不少文士纷纷逃到今江苏、浙江一带避乱，其中也包括张继。一个秋天的夜晚，诗人泊舟苏州城外的枫桥，途经寒山寺时写下了这首意境清远的羁旅诗。

"Mooring by Maple Bridge at Night" is a poem written by Zhang Ji, a Tang Dynasty poet. After the outbreak of An-Shi Rebellion, Emperor Xuanzong fled to Shu (Sichuan Province) in a hurry in June of the following year. Since the political situation in the regions south of the Yangtze River was relatively stable at that time, many scholars including Zhang Ji fled to the present Jiangsu and Zhejiang areas to escape the chaos. On an autumn night, the poet wrote the drift-themed poem with a deep and quiet artistic conception when he moored by the Maple Bridge outside Suzhou City.

枫桥夜泊
张继

月落乌啼霜满天，江枫渔火对愁眠。
姑苏城外寒山寺，夜半钟声到客船。

Mooring by Maple Bridge at Night
Zhang Ji

At moonset cry the crows, streaking the frosty sky;

Dimly lit fishing boats 'neath maples sadly lie.

Beyond the city wall, from Temple of Cold Hill

Bells break the ship-borne roamer's dream and midnight still.

全诗前两句意象密集，通过月亮落下、乌鸦啼叫、寒气满天、江边枫树、渔火、不眠旅人等，营造出一种意蕴浓郁的情境。首句"月落""乌啼""霜满天"描写诗人的所见、所闻、所感，层次分明地体现出一个先后承接的时间过程和感觉过程，并和谐地统一于水乡秋夜的幽寂清冷氛围和羁旅者的孤寂清寥感受之中。第二句通过"江枫""渔火"这样一静一动、一暗一明、岸上与江边的描写，将景物十分巧妙地配搭组合，"对愁眠"则在刻画出旅人的缕缕轻愁的同时，隐含着诗人对旅途幽美风物的新鲜感受。

The images in the first two lines are of high density, creating a rich situation through moonset, moonset, crows' crying, riverside maples, lights on fishing boats, and sleepless roamer. Moonset, the crows cry, and the frosty sky in the first line describe the poet's seeing, hearing, and feeling, clearly reflecting a sequence of time and feeling, which harmoniously blend in the quiet and cold atmosphere of the autumn night in the regions south of the Yangtze River and the loneliness of travelers. The second line depicts the scenery of maples and dimly lit fishing boats, cleverly combining the static with the dynamic, brightness with darkness, and the bank with the riverside, while "sadly lie" depicts the roamer's light sorrow, implying the poet's fresh feeling of the beautiful scenery during the journey.

后两句意象疏宕，通过"城外""寒山寺""夜半""钟声""客船"，描绘了羁旅客子卧闻静夜钟声的情景，营造出一种空灵、旷远的意境。第三句的"寒山寺"因唐初诗僧寒山曾住于此而得名，在这里增添了全诗的历史文化色彩。尾句既有仿佛回荡着历史回声的古刹钟声，给人一种古雅庄严之感，又以夜的静谧、深永和清寥衬托出诗人卧听钟声时那难以言传的感受。

The last two lines represent a clear and spacious imagery through the city, temple, midnight, bells, and ship, depicting the scene of a roamer lying and listening for the bells at night and creating an ethereal and far-flung atmosphere. "Temple of Cold Hill" in the third line was named after the monk poet Hanshan (Cold Hill) who once lived there in the early Tang Dynasty, adding a historical and cultural color to the entire poem. The last line not only gives a sense of elegance and solemnity with the ancient temple bells by which history seems to resonate, but also highlights the indescribable feeling of the poet lying and listening for the bells through the tranquility and solitude of the night.

这首诗形象鲜明，有景有情，有声有色，给人带来了枫桥的诗意美。同时，全诗以"愁"字统起，将作者的羁旅之思、家国之忧，以及身处乱世尚无归宿的顾虑充分地表现出来，创造出了情景交融的艺术意境。

With vivid images, scenery and emotions, as well as sounds and colors, this poem brings the poetic beauty of Maple Bridge to the world. At the same time, the word "sadly" dominates the entire poem, fully expressing the poet's thoughts on the journey, worries about his family and the country, and concerns about being in the troubled times without a sense of belonging, creating an artistic atmosphere with the scenery depicted and the emotions expressed in perfect harmony.

江 南 春
Spring on the Southern Rivershore

扫码看视频

杜牧生活的晚唐时代，唐王朝已不复往日的繁华。宪宗当政后，做起了长生不老的春秋大梦。他被太监杀死后，后继的穆宗、敬宗、文宗照例提倡佛教。僧尼之数继续上升，寺院经济持续发展，大大削弱了政府的实力，加重了国家的负担。

The late Tang Dynasty that Du Mu lived in was no longer as prosperous as before. After Xianzong came to power, he dreamed of immortality. After he was killed by an eunuch, his successors—Muzong, Jingzong and Wenzong advocated Buddhism as usual, so the number of monks and nuns continued to rise, and the temple economy continuously developed, which had greatly weakened the strength of the government and increased the burden of the state.

杜牧这年来到江南，不禁想起当年南朝事佛虔诚，到头来却是一场空。统治者不仅没有求得长生，反而误国害民。这首诗既是咏史怀古，也是对唐王朝统治者委婉的劝诫。后来武宗发动会昌灭佛（公元 845 年），在一定程度上缓和了矛盾。

When Du Mu came to the south of the Yangtze River this year, he could not help thinking of the piety for the Buddha in the Southern Dynasty. In the end, it was all in vain. The ruler did not obtained eternal life, but harmed the country and the people. The poem was not only a reminder of history, but also a euphemistic exhortation to the rulers of the Tang Dynasty. Later, Emperor Wuzong demolished the Buddhism in the fifth year of Huichang (845

CE), which eased the conflict to a certain extent.

江 南 春

杜牧

千里莺啼绿映红，

水村山郭酒旗风。

南朝四百八十寺，

多少楼台烟雨中。

Spring on the Southern Rivershore

Du Mu

Orioles sing for miles amid red blooms and green trees;

By hills and rills wine shop streamers wave in the breeze.

Four hundred eighty splendid temples still remain

Of Southern Dynasties in the mist and rain.

　　《江南春》是唐代诗人杜牧创作的一首七言绝句。诗中不仅描绘了明媚的江南春光，而且再现了江南烟雨蒙蒙的楼台景色，诗中江南风光神奇迷离，别有一番情趣。这首诗有众多意象和景物，有植物、有动物，有声有色，景物也有远近之分，动静结合，各具特色。全诗以轻快的文字和极具概括性的语言描绘了一幅生动形象、丰富多彩而又有气势的江南春画卷，呈现出一种深邃幽美的意境，表达出一缕缕含蓄深蕴的情思，千百年来素负盛名。

　　"Spring on the Southern Rivershore" is a seven-character quatrain written by Du Mu, a poet of the Tang Dynasty. The poem not only depicts the bright spring scenery of southern China, but also reproduces the scenery of temples in the mist and rain, making the scenery of southern China more magical and mysterious, which is quite interesting. There are many images and scenes in this poem—plants and animals, sounds and colors, long shots and close-ups, combining movement with standstill, each of which has its own characteristics. The whole poem describes a vivid, colorful and imposing picture of spring in southern China with light words and very general language, showing a profound, secluded and beautiful artistic conception, expressing a kind of implicit and profound feelings, which has had a high reputation for thousands of years.

泊 秦 淮
Moored on River Qinhuai

扫码看视频

　　杜牧颇为关心政治，他看到唐王朝统治集团的腐朽昏庸、藩镇的拥兵自固、边患的频繁，深感社会危机四伏，唐王朝前景可悲。这种感时伤世的思想，促使他写了许多具有现实意义的诗篇，《泊秦淮》就是其中之一。

　　Du Mu was quite concerned about politics. He saw the corruption and incompetence of the ruling administration of the Tang Dynasty, the military governor's self-preservation, and the frequent border conflicts. Therefore, he felt deeply that social crises were everywhere, and the future of the Tang Dynasty was bleak. This melancholic and sorrowful attitude towards the world prompted him to write many poems with practical significance, among which "Moored on River Qinhuai" was one.

泊 秦 淮
杜牧

烟笼寒水月笼沙，

夜泊秦淮近酒家。

商女不知亡国恨，

隔江犹唱后庭花。

Moored on River Qinhuai
Du Mu

Cold water and sand bars veiled in misty moonlight,

I moor on River Qinhuai near wineshops at night.

The songstress knows not the grief of the captive king,

By riverside she sings his song of Parting Spring.

《泊秦淮》是杜牧夜泊秦淮时触景感怀之作，前半段写秦淮夜景，后半段抒发感慨，借南朝陈后主因追求荒淫享乐终至亡国的历史，讽刺那些不以国事为重、只顾寻欢作乐的晚唐统治者，表现了诗人对国家命运的无比关怀和深切忧虑的情怀。全诗寓情于景，意境悲凉，感情深沉含蓄，语言精练形象，构思细密精巧，写景、抒情、叙事有机结合，具有强烈的艺术感染力。

"Moored on River Qinhuai" is a poem written by Du Mu, who was moved by the scenery while traveling along the Qinhuai River at night. The first half of the poem depicts the night view of the Qinhuai River, while the second half expresses the poet's profound sentiments and draws on the history of Chen Shubao, the last emperor of the Chen Dynasty, whose obsession with indulgence ultimately led to the downfall of his kingdom. It satirizes the late Tang Dynasty rulers who prioritized trivial pleasures over national affairs, using the theme of a collapsing empire to criticize their pursuit of revelry. It displays the poet's immense concern and deep anxiety for the destiny of the nation. The whole poem imbues

emotions within scenery, evoking a bleak and desolate atmosphere with profound and restrained sentiments. The language is concise and vivid, whereas the conception is intricate and exquisite. The integration of scene depiction, emotional expression, and narrative is seamless, possessing a strong artistic appeal.

雨霖铃 · 寒蝉凄切
Bells Ringing in the Rain

扫码看视频

这是宋代词人柳永从汴京（今河南开封）南下与一位恋人惜别时创作的作品，读起来如行云流水，起伏跌宕中不见雕琢的痕迹。

"Bells Ringing in the Rain" was written by the poet Liu Yong of the Song Dynasty when he bid farewell to a lover on his way south from the capital Bianjing (now Kaifeng in Henan Province). With a freely flowing style of writing, it rises and falls naturally without trace of carving.

雨霖铃 · 寒蝉凄切
柳永

寒蝉凄切，对长亭晚，骤雨初歇。都门帐饮无绪，留恋处，兰舟催发。执手相看泪眼，竟无语凝噎。念去去，千里烟波，暮霭沉沉楚天阔。

多情自古伤离别，更那堪冷落清秋节！今宵酒醒何处？杨柳岸，晓风残月。此去经年，应是良辰好景虚设。便纵有千种风情，更与何人说？

Bells Ringing in the Rain
Liu Yong

Cicadas chill

Drearily shrill.

We stand face to face in an evening hour

Before the pavilion, after a sudden shower.

Can we care for drinking before we part?

At the city gate we are lingering late,

But the boat is waiting for me to depart.

Hand in hand we gaze at each other's tearful eyes

And burst into sobs with words congealed on our lips.

I'll go my way, far, far away.

On miles and miles of misty waves where sail ships,

And evening clouds hang low in boundless Southern skies.

Lovers would grieve at parting as of old.

How could I stand this clear autumn day so cold!

Where shall I be found at daybreak

From wine awake?

Moored by a riverbank planted with willow trees

Beneath the waning moon and in the morning breeze.

I'll be gone for a year.

In vain would good times and fine scenes appear.

However gallant I am on my part,

To whom can I lay bare my heart?

词的上阕细致刻画了一对恋人饯行时难舍难分的场景，抒发了离情别绪。起首一句写别时正当秋季，景已萧瑟，且值天晚，暮色阴沉，而骤雨滂沱之后，继之以寒蝉凄切。词人所见所闻无处不凄凉，为后一句的"无绪"和"催发"设下伏笔。恋人在都门外长亭摆下酒筵给词人送别，然而词人面对美酒佳肴却毫无兴致，留恋情浓与兰舟催发的矛盾冲突将离别之紧迫、情人之难舍难分表现得淋漓尽致，于是便有了"执手相看泪眼，竟无语凝噎"一句。词人凝噎在喉的是"念去去"一句的内心独白：在如此广阔辽远的空间里，充满了浓密深沉的烟霭。其离愁之深，令人可以想见。

The first half of the poem depicts delicately the scene of a pair of lovers who were reluctant to part when having a farewell dinner, expressing the feelings of parting. In the beginning, it depicts a desolate scene as they parted in autumn. Since it was in an evening hour, evening clouds hung low. Cicadas chill drearily shrilled after a sudden shower. What the poet saw and heard was desolate everywhere, foreshadowing "(not) care for" and "waiting to depart" in the following two lines. The lover gave a farewell dinner before the pavilion outside the city gate, but they did not care for drinking. They were lingering until it was late, but the boat was waiting to depart. The poem vividly depicts the urgency of departure time and the reluctance to say goodbye to lovers. So there is: "Hand in hand we gaze at each other's tearful eyes, And burst into sobs with

words congealed on our lips." The words congealed on the poet's lips were his inner monologue of the next two lines: Mist and clouds were so thick in such boundless skies, by which you can imagine how painful their parting was.

词的下阕着重摹写想象中别后的凄楚情状。先言伤离惜别这一人生哲理,"更那堪"加强了感情色彩,突出在冷落凄凉的秋季离情更甚。"今宵"两句描写了客情之冷落、风景之清幽、离愁之绵邈,画面充满了凄清的气氛。"此去经年"两句构成另一种情境:相聚之日,每逢良辰好景,总感到欢娱,可是别后相爱的人不在一起,纵有良辰好景也不能引起欣赏的兴致,即使有满腔的情意又能向谁诉说呢?以问句作结,更留有无穷意味,耐人寻味。

The second half of the poem focuses on depicting the grief after the imaginary parting. It begins with the life philosophy that lovers would grieve at parting, and intensifies the emotion with "How could I stand", highlighting that the grief of parting would be magnified in such a cold autumn day. The following four lines (in translation) depict the desolation of the traveller, the serenity of the scenery, and the deep sorrow of parting, creating a picture full of melancholic atmosphere. The last four lines (in translation) create another scenario: On the day of gathering, we feel happy in every good time and enjoy fine scene; but after parting, all these would appear to be in vain. Even if full of gallantry, "to whom can I lay bare my heart?" Ended with a question, it is profoundly meaningful and intriguing.

全词围绕"伤离别"而构思,先写离别之前,重在勾勒环境;次写离别时刻,重在描写情态;再写别后想象,重在刻画心理。做到前后照应,虚实相生,层层深入,尽情描绘,情景交融,蕴藉深沉,将情人惜别时的真情实感表达得缠绵悱恻、凄婉动人,堪称抒写别情的千古名篇,也是柳词和婉约词的代表作。

The entire poem centers on "grieve at parting". Before parting, it emphasizes the depiction of the surroundings. At the moment of parting, it emphasizes the portrayal of mental and physical activities. Then it depicts the imaginary parting, emphasizing the portrayal of mental states. The correlation between ending and beginning, the combination of nihility and reality, the unrestrained depictions with great depth, the blending of scenes and emotions, and the implicitness and refinedness, all express the lovers' true feelings when parting in a sentimental way, making it one of the most famous literary works in portraying parting, as well as a masterpiece of Liu Yong's poems and the graceful and restrained poems.

渔家傲·秋思
Tune: Fisherman's Pride

扫码看视频

范仲淹是北宋著名的军事家、政治家、文学家。他了解民间疾苦，深知宋王朝在政治、经济、军事等方面存在的问题，主张革除积弊，但因统治集团内部守旧派的反对，所以没能实现。

Fan Zhongyan was a famous militarist, politician and litterateur in the Northern Song Dynasty. He understood the hardships of the people and was well aware of the problems that existed in politics, economy, military, and other aspects of the Song Dynasty. He advocated for the elimination of accumulated malpractice, but due to opposition from the conservative factions within the ruling group, it was not possible to achieve this.

这首《渔家傲·秋思》是范仲淹的代表作，反映了他亲身经历的边塞生活。词人用近乎白描的手法，在上片描摹出了一幅寥廓荒僻、萧瑟悲凉的边塞鸟瞰图；下片则抒发了边关将士壮志难酬和思乡忧国的情怀。整首词反映了边塞生活的艰苦和词人巩固边防的决心与意愿，同时还表现出外患未除、功业未建、厌战思归等复杂、矛盾的情感。

The "Tune: Fisherman's Pride" is Fan Zhongyan's representative work, reflecting his own experience of frontier life. The poet used a technique of almost line drawing to depict a desolate bird's-eye view of the frontier fortress on the first part. The second part expresses the heroic aspirations of border soldiers and their homesickness and concerns for the country. The entire poem reflects the hardships of border life and the determination and willingness of the poet to consolidate border defense. At the same time, it also expresses complex and contradictory emotions for unresolved external threats, unfinished achievements, tiredness of war and yearning for home.

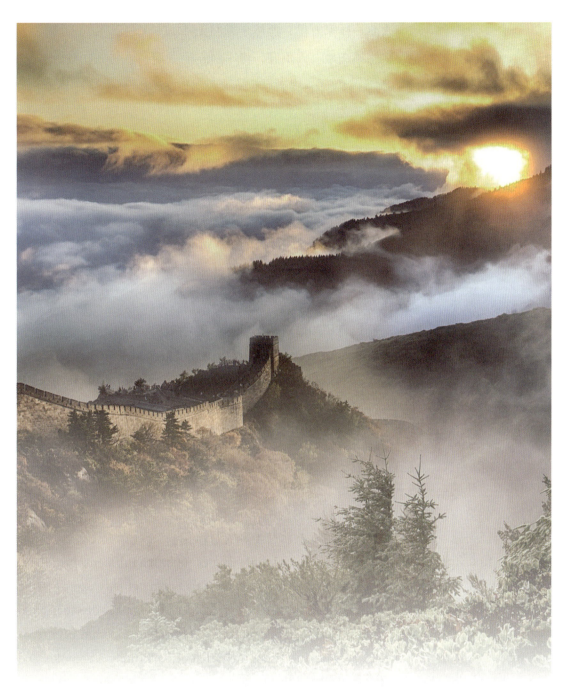

渔家傲·秋思

范仲淹

塞下秋来风景异，衡阳雁去无留意。

四面边声连角起，千嶂里，长烟落日孤城闭。

浊酒一杯家万里，燕然未勒归无计。

羌管悠悠霜满地，人不寐，将军白发征夫泪。

Tune: Fisherman's Pride

Fan Zhongyan

When autumn comes to the frontier, the scene looks drear;

Southbound wild geese won't stay e'en for a day.

An uproar rises with horns blowing far and near.

Walled in by peaks, smoke rises straight

At sunset over isolate town with closed gate.

I hold a cup of wine, yet home is far away;

The northwest not yet won, I can't but stay.

At the flutes' doleful sound over frost-covered ground,

None falls asleep,

The general's hair turns white and soldiers weep.

　　《渔家傲·秋思》这首词首先给人的感觉是凄清、悲凉、壮阔、深沉，有些伤感，也回荡着悲壮的英雄气。这首词既表现出了将军的英雄气概及征途的艰苦生活，也暗寓对宋王朝重内轻外政策的不满。将军的爱国激情和浓重的思乡之情兼而有之，构成了将军与征夫思乡却渴望建功立业的复杂而又矛盾的心情。

　　The first impression given by the poem is bleak, desolate, magnificent, profound, somewhat sad, and also echoing a heroic and tragic spirit. This poem not only expresses the heroic spirit of the general and the difficult life on the journey, but also implies dissatisfaction with the Song Dynasty's policy of prioritizing internal affairs over external affairs. It combines the general's patriotic passion and strong homesickness, forming a complex and contradictory mood between the general and the conscripts who yearn for home but aspire to achieve success.

泊 船 瓜 洲
Moored at the Ferry

扫码看视频

《泊船瓜洲》是北宋文学家王安石创作的一首七言绝句。人们对其具体写作时间存有争议，主要有三种观点：其一认为此诗是在宋神宗熙宁元年（公元 1068 年），王安石应召自江宁府（今南京）赴京任翰林学士，途经瓜洲时所作；其二认为此诗是在宋神宗熙宁七年（公元 1074 年），王安石第一次罢相自京还江宁，途径瓜洲时所作；其三认为此诗是在宋神宗熙宁八年（公元 1075 年），王安石第二次拜相，自江宁赴京途经瓜洲时所作。

"Moored at the Ferry" is a seven-character quatrain poem written by Wang Anshi, a literary figure from the Northern Song Dynasty. The exact time of its creation is a matter of dispute, with three main viewpoints: The first viewpoint suggests that this poem was composed in the first year of the Xining reign (1068 CE) of Emperor Shenzong of Song. Wang Anshi, being summoned to serve as a scholar in the Hanlin Academy in the capital, wrote the poem while passing through Guazhou. The second viewpoint suggests that this poem was written in the seventh year of the Xining reign (1074 CE) when Wang Anshi was first dismissed from his position as the prime minister and returned from the capital to Jiangning. He wrote the poem during his journey through Guazhou.

The third viewpoint suggests that this poem was composed in the eighth year of the Xining reign (1075 CE) when Wang Anshi was appointed as the prime minister for the second time. He wrote the poem while traveling from Jiangning to the capital and passing through Guazhou.

全诗以景开篇，又兼具比兴手法，通过夸张将空间上的近与时间上的久构成了有力的反差，以诗抒情，以景传感，最终以结句"明月何时照我还"的情感迸发，让人回味无穷。

The poem begins with a description of the scenery, employing the technique of analogy and association to create a strong contrast between the proximity in space and the distance in time in an exaggerated way. The poet expresses emotions and conveys sensations through the use of poetic and scenic imagery. Ultimately, the poem culminates with the emotional outburst of the closing line, "When will the moon shine bright on my return?", leaving a lasting impression.

泊船瓜洲

王安石

京口瓜洲一水间，

钟山只隔数重山。

春风又绿江南岸，

明月何时照我还。

Moored at the Ferry

Wang Anshi

A river severs northern shore and southern land,

Between my home and me but a few mountains stand.

The vernal wind has greened the southern shore again,

When will the moon shine bright on my return? O when?

　　全诗以"泊船瓜洲"为题，借诗人所见之景，描绘诗人心中所感。第一句通过"一水间"三字写京口和瓜洲距离之短及行船之快，流露出一种轻松、愉悦的心情。第二句写诗人回望居住地钟山，以"只隔"二字言钟山近在咫尺却被"数重山"挡住，暗示诗人归心似箭。第三句描写了春意盎然的江南景色，其中"绿"字用得绝妙。传说王安石为了用好这个字足足改了十多次，最后以"绿"字开拓全诗景色塑造的新形象，表达了春风吹过以后千里江岸一片新绿的景物变化，把看不见的春风转换成鲜明的视觉形象，以此寄托诗人浩荡的情思。尾句用疑问的句式，描绘诗人眺望已久的情境。随着红日西沉，夜色悄然而至，隔岸景色已渐渐消失在朦胧月色中，诗人对钟山的思念之感越发强烈，全诗进一步表达了诗人的思乡之情。全诗不仅寓情于景，借景抒情，写景于静，而且以"绿"化动，从而在叙事上也富有情致，境界开阔，格调清新，耐人寻味。

Titled "Moored at the Ferry", the poem depicts the poet's inner thoughts through the scenery he sees. The first line highlights the short distance between Jingkou and Guazhou and the fast speed of boat by using the three Chinese characters "一水间", conveying a feeling of ease and pleasure. In the second line, the poet looks back at his home, Zhongshan, and uses the two Chinese characters "只隔" to suggest that although Zhongshan is nearby, it is blocked by "a few mountains", implying that the poet's heart is set on returning home as soon as possible. The third line describes the flourishing scenery of Jiangnan (the south of the Yangtze River) in spring, with the Chinese character "绿" being used exceptionally well. Legend has it that Wang Anshi revised the line for more than ten times to find a perfect Chinese character as an effective verb, ultimately creating a new image of the scenery throughout the poem. This portrays the transformation of the landscape into a vibrant green after being stirred by the spring breeze, converting the invisible breeze into a vivid visual image, symbolizing the poet's deep emotions. The final line uses the interrogative line to depict the poet's long gaze. As the red sun sets and the night falls, the scenery across the river gradually disappears in the misty moonlight. The poet's yearning for his homeland is intensified, and the poem expresses the poet's homesickness in a further way. The entire poem not only embodies emotions within the scenery, expressing sentiments through the depiction of landscapes, but also captures the dynamic essence through using "green" as a verb. As a result, the narrative is imbued with a poetic sentiment, offering a broadened perspective and a fresh style that is thought-provoking.

水调歌头·明月几时有
Prelude to Water Melody

扫码看视频

中秋佳节，皓月当空，苏轼与弟弟分别已七年有余。他对弟弟的思念越发强烈，于是借中秋夜的一轮明月，抒发自己对亲人的思念和美好祝愿，同时也表达了自己虽仕途不顺但仍然乐观豁达的精神。

On the Mid-Autumn Festival, the bright moon hung high in the sky, and it had been more than seven years since Su Shi and his younger brother were separated. The poet's yearning for his younger brother became increasingly strong, so with the bright moon of the Mid-Autumn Festival, he expressed his yearning and best wishes for his family members as well as his optimistic and open-minded spirit even though his career was not going well.

水调歌头·明月几时有

苏轼

明月几时有？把酒问青天。

不知天上宫阙，今夕是何年。

我欲乘风归去，又恐琼楼玉宇，高处不胜寒。

起舞弄清影，何似在人间。

转朱阁，低绮户，照无眠。

不应有恨，何事长向别时圆？

人有悲欢离合，月有阴晴圆缺，此事古难全。

但愿人长久，千里共婵娟。

Prelude to Water Melody

Su Shi

How long will the full moon appear?

Wine cup in hand, I ask the sky.

I do not know what time of year,

It would be tonight in the palace on high.

Riding the wind, there I would fly,

yet I'm afraid the crystalline palace would be too high and cold for me.

I rise and dance, with my shadow I play.

On high as on earth, would it be as gay?

The moon goes round the mansions red.

Through gauze-draped windows to shed Her light upon the sleepless bed.

Against man she should have no spite.

Why then when people part, is she oft full and bright?

Men have sorrow and joy, they meet or part again;

The moon is bright or dim and she may wax or wane. There has been nothing perfect since

the olden days, so let us wish that man

May live long as he can!

Though miles apart, we'll share the beauty she displays.

诗人上阕望月，寄思想于天宫之上，下阕思念亲人，然而结尾却一扫思念的阴霾，表明虽无法团聚，思念之情却相通。这首词是后世中秋望月怀人之佳作。

In the first stanza, gazing at the moon, the poet's thoughts are projected to the heavenly kingdom. In the second stanza, feelings of longing for one's family members are expressed. Yet, the ending dispels the gloom of separation, expressing that while reunion may not be possible, the bond of affection remains unbroken. This ci poem is a masterpiece of later generations' works that praise the moon and express sentiments of longing for distant loved ones during the Mid-Autumn Festival.

念奴娇·赤壁怀古
Tune: Charm of a Maiden Singer · Memories of the Past at Red Cliff

扫码看视频

　　《念奴娇·赤壁怀古》是宋代文学家苏轼的词作，是豪放词的代表作之一。此词通过对月夜江上壮美景色的描绘，以及借对古代战场的凭吊和对风流人物的才略、气度、功业的追念，曲折地表现了词人怀才不遇、功业未就、壮志未酬的忧愤之情，同时表现了词人的旷达之心。

　　"Tune: Charm of a Maiden Singer · Memories of the Past at Red Cliff" is a masterpiece of Su Shi, a litterateur of the Song Dynasty, and it is one of the representative works of

132

poetry in a bold and unconstrained style. Through the depiction of the magnificent scenery of the Great River on a moonlit night, and the commemoration of the ancient battlefield and the heroes' ability and sagacity, magnanimity and achievements, it circuitously expresses the poet's melancholy and indignation for his unrecognized talents, unfinished cause and unrealized achievements, while also revealing the poet's broad-mindedness.

念奴娇·赤壁怀古

苏轼

大江东去，浪淘尽，千古风流人物。

故垒西边，人道是，三国周郎赤壁。

乱石穿空，惊涛拍岸，卷起千堆雪。

江山如画，一时多少豪杰。

遥想公瑾当年，小乔初嫁了，雄姿英发。

羽扇纶巾，谈笑间，樯橹灰飞烟灭。

故国神游，多情应笑我，早生华发。

人生如梦，一尊还酹江月。

Tune: Charm of a Maiden Singer · Memories of the Past at Red Cliff

Su Shi

The Great River eastward flows,

With its waves are gone all those

Gallant heroes of bygone years.

West of the ancient fortress appears

The Red Cliff. Here General Zhou won his early fame

When the Three Kingdoms were all in flame.

Jagged rocks tower in the air,

Swashing waves beat on the shore,

Rolling up a thousand heaps of snow.

To match the hills and the river so fair,

How many heroes brave of yore

Made a great show!

I fancy General Zhou at the height

Of his success,

With a plume fan in hand,

In a silk hood, so brave and bright,

Laughing and jesting with his bride so fair,

While enemy ships were destroyed as planned

Like shadowy castles in the air.

Should their souls revisit this land,

Sentimental, his wife would laugh to say,

Younger than they, I have my hair all turned grey.

Life is but like a passing dream,

I'd drink to the moon which once saw them on the stream.

此词乃为怀古抒情所作。元丰三年（1080 年），苏轼被贬为小小的黄州（今湖北黄冈）团练副使，仕途暗淡。诗人游览赤壁山，上阕写自己被自然的风景所震撼，由此联想到赤壁之战，揭开下阕对周郎等的描写，从而联想到自身。古代豪杰拥有雄心壮志，诗人恨自己不能建功立业，壮志难酬。本诗最后抒发积极进取、旷达奋进之情，是豪放词的代表作。

This poem is a work of nostalgic sentiment. In the third year of the Yuanfeng (1080 CE), Su Shi was demoted to the humble position of vice instructor of the Huangzhou (present-day Huanggang, Hubei) militia, and his political career was bleak. He visited the Red Cliff and was struck by the nature scenery, which led to his reflections on the Battle of Red Cliff, opening the second part with descriptions of Zhou Yu and others, and hence reflecting on himself. The ancient heroes had grand ambitions, and the poet lamented his own inability to achieve great deeds, his aspirations unfulfilled. In the end the poem expresses the feelings of being enterprising and open-minded, and is regarded as a masterpiece of unconstrained ci school.

一剪梅·红藕香残玉簟秋
A Twig of Mume Blossoms
To the Tune of a Spray of Flowering Plum

扫码看视频

这首词是宋代女词人李清照前期的作品，通常被认为是李清照写给丈夫赵明诚的相思之作。李清照婚后不久，丈夫赵明诚出门游学。在与丈夫离别之后，词人用曲折婉转的细腻笔触描写了夫妻情爱中的离愁别绪，寄寓她不忍离别的一腔深情，给人一种淡淡的凄美之感。

This ci poem is an early work of Li Qingzhao, a poetess of the Song Dynasty. It is usually regarded as a love poem for her husband Zhao Mingcheng. Shortly after marriage, her husband went on a study tour. After parting from her husband, the poetess described the sorrow of parting between a loving couple with tortuous and delicate strokes, conveying the deep feeling that she could not bear to be parted, which gave a subtle sense of sadness and beauty.

一剪梅·红藕香残玉簟秋
李清照

红藕香残玉簟秋。

轻解罗裳，独上兰舟。云中谁寄锦书来？

雁字回时，月满西楼。

花自飘零水自流。

一种相思，两处闲愁。

此情无计可消除，才下眉头，却上心头。

A Twig of Mume Blossoms
To the Tune of a Spray of Flowering Plum
Li Qingzhao

When autumn chills my mat, the fragrant lotus fade.

My silk robe doffed, I float

Alone in orchid boat.

Who in the cloud would bring me letters in brocade?

When wild geese come, I'll wait

At moonlit bower's gate.

As flowers fall on running water here as there,

I am longing for thee

Just as thou art for me.

How can such sorrow be driven away fore'er?

From eyebrows kept apart,

Again it gnaws my heart.

　　词的上阕主要写了词人在这一天内的行为和感受，包括白天的悠闲时光和夜晚抬头望月的感慨。起句领起全篇，上半句"红藕香残"写户外之景，下半句"玉簟秋"写室内之物，点出清秋季节天气转凉，借户内外景物暗寓情意，营造这首词的环境气氛和感情色彩。接下来的五句按时间顺序写词人从昼到夜一天内所做之事、所触之景、所生之情。"轻解罗裳，独上兰舟"描写白天在水面泛舟之事，以"独上"暗示离情。"云中谁寄锦书来"则明写别后的悬念，回应上句舟中所望所思，并引出雁足传书的遐想和月夜遥望星空的情思。

　　The first half of the poem mainly describes the poetess actions and feelings in a day, including the leisurely time during the day and the feeling of looking up at the moon at night. The first line sets the tone for the whole poem, with "the fragrant lotus fade" depicting outdoor scenery and "when autumn chills my mat" depicting indoor items, pointing out that the weather turns cool in autumn. Emotions are implied in the description of indoor and outdoor scenery, which creates the environmental atmosphere and emotional color of the poem. The next five lines are written in the order of what the poetess did, what she saw, and what she felt from day to night. "My silk robe doffed, I float alone in orchid boat." describes her boating during the day, while "alone" implies her feeling of parting. "Who in the cloud would bring me letters in brocade?" depicts the suspense after parting, responding to what she saw and thought on the boat in the above line and leading to the reverie of wild geese' delivering letters and the mood of gazing at the stars in the moonlit night.

　　词的下阕则是词人对可能收到丈夫书信的期待，以及对过去美好时光的回忆。"花自飘零水自流"承上启下，既描写了花落水流之景，也暗含人生、年华、爱情、离别之感。后五句转为直抒胸臆——"一种相思，两处闲愁"，既表达了词人的相思之苦、闲愁之深，也表明了词人与丈夫的情爱之笃和信任之深。"此情无计可消除"则表达了夫妻分在两处，心已笼罩深愁，此情难以排遣，因此"才下眉头，却上心头"，将词人对丈夫深深的思念和她哀而不伤的中和气质表现得淋漓尽致。

The latter half of the poem describes the poetess' expectation of receiving a letter from her husband, and the memory of the good times in the past. "As flowers fall on running water here as there" serves as a connecting link between the preceding and the following. It not only describes the scene of flowers' falling on running water, but also implies multiple emotions about the flow of time, the journey of life and the sense of love and parting. The last five lines shift to expressions directly—"I am longing for thee, just as thou art for me." It not only expresses the poetess' lovesickness and deep longing, but also shows their sincere love and deep trust. "How can such sorrow be driven away fore'er?" shows that since the couple parted, their hearts had been shrouded in a deep sorrow which was difficult to be driven away, so "From eyebrows kept apart, again it gnaws my heart", which incisively and vividly conveys the poetess' deep longing for her husband and her moderate temperament of being mournful but not distressing.

这首词格调清新，巧妙运用时间和空间转换，人物情感描写细腻，反映了词人的内心世界，也展现了词人高雅的艺术品位和忠贞的爱情观。

In a fresh style, this poem makes good use of the change of time and space, and describes the emotions of the characters delicately, reflecting the inner world of the poetess, and showing her elegant artistic taste and loyalty to love.

声声慢·寻寻觅觅
Slow Sound · Seek and Find

扫码看视频

纵观古今，李清照可以说是"千古第一女词人"，这一评价足以彰显李清照写词的功力。处于和平时期的李清照写得更多的是对爱情的追求与抒怀。相比前期的懵懂和爱慕，李清照创作后期的作品再没有当年的那种清新可人、浅斟低唱，而转为沉郁凄婉，主要抒写她对亡夫赵明诚的怀念和自己孤单凄凉的景况。《声声慢·寻寻觅觅》

便是这一时期的典型代表作品之一。

To take a panoramic view from ancient times to present society, Li Qingzhao can be said to be the first ci poetess throughout the ages, and this evaluation mirrors Li Qingzhao's competence to write poems. In peacetime, Li Qingzhao wrote more poems about the pursuit and expression of love. Compared with the ignorance and admiration in the early works, her later ones were no longer that fresh and pleasant. Instead, they became melancholy and pathetic, mainly expressing her memory of her late husband Zhao Mingcheng and her own lonely and desolate situation. The poem "Slow Sound · Seek and Find" is one of the typical works of this period.

声声慢·寻寻觅觅

李清照

寻寻觅觅，冷冷清清，凄凄惨惨戚戚。

乍暖还寒时候，最难将息。

三杯两盏淡酒，怎敌他、晚来风急！

雁过也，正伤心，却是旧时相识。

满地黄花堆积，憔悴损，如今有谁堪摘？

守着窗儿，独自怎生得黑！

梧桐更兼细雨，到黄昏、点点滴滴。

这次第，怎一个愁字了得！

Slow Sound · Seek and Find

Li Qingzhao

So dim, so dark,

So dense, so dull,

So damp, so dank,

So dead!

The weather, now warm, now cold,

Makes it harder

Than ever to forget!

How can a few cups of thin wine

Bring warmth against

The chilly winds of sunset?

I recognize the geese flying overhead:

My old friends,

Bring not the old memories back!

Let fallen flowers lie where they fall.

To what purpose

And for whom should I decorate?

By the window shut,

Guarding it alone,

To see the sky has turned so black!

And the drizzle on the kolanut

Keeps on droning:

Pit-a-pat, pit-a-pat!

Is this the kind of mood and moment

To be expressed

By one word "sad"?

　　起句连用七组叠词，把宋词的音调和谐运用到了极致，以"寻寻觅觅"表示词人的孤落寂寞。"乍暖还寒时候"表面是写天气，实际上却巧妙地对应了词人当时的处境。"最难将息"则与上文"寻寻觅觅"相呼应，说明词人从一清早就不知如何是好。

　　Starting with seven groups of repeated words, it applies the phonological harmony of Song poems to the extreme, with "寻寻觅觅" displaying her loneliness. "乍暖还寒时候" is written on the surface of the weather, but actually corresponds to the situation at that time. "最难将息" echoes with the above "寻寻觅觅", indicating that she didn't know what to do from the early morning.

　　接下来的"三杯两盏淡酒，怎敌他、晚来风急！"，正与上文"乍暖还寒"相合，是说借酒消愁是不抵事的。上阕从一个人寻觅无着，写到酒难浇愁，雁过伤心，增加了思乡的惆怅；下阕则由秋日高空转入自家庭院，园中开满了菊花，秋意正浓。

The following "三杯两盏淡酒，怎敌他、晚来风急！" is in concert with the above "乍暖还寒", meaning that it was no good drinking down sorrow. The first half of the poem begins from the poetess's seeking alone for nothing, finding she could not drink her sadness away, to the flying geese, which increased the melancholy of homesickness; the second half writes from the autumn sky to the yard full of chrysanthemums, where autumn was very much in the air.

"满地黄花堆积"是指菊花盛开，而非残英满地。"憔悴损"暗指词人因忧伤而憔悴瘦损。正由于词人无心看花，所以虽值菊花满地，词人也不想去摘它、赏它，这才是"如今有谁堪摘"的确解。然而人不摘花，花当自萎，但等到花已损，则欲摘已不堪摘了。这里既写出了词人无心摘花的郁闷，又表露了其惜花将谢的情怀。

"满地黄花堆积" refers to chrysanthemums in full bloom instead of the fallen flowers. "憔悴损" implies that she was emaciated with grief. Just because she was in no mood for seeing flowers, she did not want to pick and enjoy them, though chrysanthemums were everywhere, which exactly explains "如今有谁堪摘". However, flowers got withered though not picked, and it was too late to pick them when they were fading away. Here it reveals not only her depression of being in no mood for picking flowers, but also her pity for the fading flowers.

破阵子·为陈同甫赋壮词以寄之
Dance of the Cavalry

扫码看视频

　　这首词作于辛弃疾因失意而闲居信州（今江西上饶）之时。宋孝宗淳熙十五年（公元 1188 年）冬天，在与陈亮（字"同甫"）的第二次"鹅湖之会"期间，辛弃疾以"破阵子"为词牌名，通过追忆早年抗金部队的阵容气概及自己的沙场生涯，表达了杀敌报国、收复失地的理想，抒发了壮志难酬、英雄迟暮的悲愤心情。

　　This ci poem was composed by Xin Qiji when he was frustrated, living idly in Xinzhou (now Shangrao, Jiangxi Province). In the winter of the 15th year of Chunxi under the reign of Emperor Xiaozong of the Song Dynasty (1188 CE), during the second path-breaking debate with Chen Liang (also known as "Tongfu"), Xin Qiji took "Dance of the Cavalry" as the name of the tune and the poem. By recalling the battle array and heroic mettle of the early anti-Jin aggression army and his own career on the battlefield, it conveyed his ideal of defeating the enemy to serve the country and regain the lost land, expressing his grief and indignation for being unable to achieve his ambition as a hero in his twilight years.

破阵子·为陈同甫赋壮词以寄之

辛弃疾

醉里挑灯看剑，梦回吹角连营。

八百里分麾下炙，五十弦翻塞外声，沙场秋点兵。

马作的卢飞快，弓如霹雳弦惊。

了却君王天下事，赢得生前身后名。可怜白发生！

Dance of the Cavalry

Xin Qiji

Though drunk, we lit the lamp to see the glaive;

Sober, we heard the horns from tent to tent.

Under the flags, beef grilled

Was eaten by our warriors brave

And martial airs were played by fifty instruments:

'T was an autumn manoeuvre in the field.

On gallant steed,

Running full speed,

We'd shoot with twanging bows

Recovering the lost land for the sovereign,

'T is everlasting fame that we would win. But alas!

White hair grows!

　　词的上阕十分生动地描绘出一位披肝沥胆、勇往直前的将军形象，表现了词人的远大抱负。首句六个字用三个富有特征性的动作，塑造了一个壮士的形象，意味无穷。壮志未酬的词人在友人纵谈离去之后，借酒浇愁愁更愁，他拨亮油灯，拔出宝剑，醉眼蒙眬中，恍惚回到当年战斗的情境。嘹亮的号角吹遍了"连营"，广阔的土地上，战士们正在分食大块的烤肉。此时鼓瑟齐鸣，反映边塞生活的军乐雄壮震天。原来战士们正在沙场点兵。一个"连"字，透出声势之豪壮、军容之整肃。"八百里""五十弦"佳对天成，与"吹角连营"相辅相成，营造了雄浑阔大的意境。

The first half of the ci poem vividly portrays the image of a loyal, faithful and valiant general, showcasing the poet's great aspirations. The first six characters employ three distinctive actions to shape the image of a warrior, imbued with profound significance. The unfulfilled poet sought solace in wine after talking freely with his friend who then left. He lit the lamp, extracted his glaive, and in a trance, went back to the scene of the battle. The resounding horns blew "from tent to tent" on the vast land, and warriors were eating grilled beef. At this time, musical instruments were played in unison the martial airs. It was a manoeuvre in the field. The character "连" reveals the grandeur and well-disciplined demeanor of the military. The good match of "八百里" and "五十弦" is complementary to "吹角连营", jointly creating a grand and forceful artistic conception.

　　词的下阕以"的卢马"的飞驰和"霹雳弦"的巨响两个特写镜头开始，词人展开丰富的想象，化身为词里的将军，身先士卒，乘胜追杀，敌人纷纷落马，残兵败将狼狈溃退，凯歌交奏，欢天喜地，旌旗招展。刚攀上理想的高峰，忽然一个陡转"可怜白发生"，从理想的高峰跌回冷酷的现实，全词至此戛然而止，为读者留下了无尽的思绪。

The second half of the poem commences with two close-ups of the running "steed" and the "twanging bows". The poet immersed himself in a rich imagination and incarnated into the general in the poem, taking the lead and chasing after a victory. Enemies were caught and defeated and fled in confusion. The triumphant songs were played in an ecstasy of joy, and flags fluttered in the wind. However, just as he climbed up the peak of the ideal, he fell back to the harsh reality by the sudden turn of "But alas! White hair grows". The entire poem stops abruptly, leaving readers with an abundance of thoughts.

这首词基调雄壮高昂，但壮和悲、理想和现实的强烈反差，令人想到当时南宋朝廷的腐败无能，想到人民的水深火热，想到所有爱国志士报国无门的苦闷。读起来波澜起伏，跌宕有致，实为辛弃疾"沉郁顿挫"的典型之作。

The tone of this poem is grand and lofty, but the strong contrasts between grandeur and sorrow, and ideals and reality, remind us of the corrupt and incompetent Southern Song Dynasty court at that time, the plight of the people, and the suffering of all patriots yearning for serving the country. With ups and downs, it is a typical work reflecting Xin Qiji's depression and frustration.

小桃红·采莲女
Tune: Red Peach Blossoms · The Lotus Gatherer

扫码看视频

这是金末元初散曲作家杨果创作的一组散曲。此组曲共包括四首散曲，描写主人公独宿江楼，被采莲人的歌声唤起，歌声触动了他对于亡国的悲痛及因国家易主而泪下的场景。

This is a group of sanqu poems created by Yang Guo, a poet in the late Jin and early Yuan dynasties. Comprising four pieces, it depicts that the protagonist slept alone in the river tower and was awakened by the singing of the lotus gatherers, which aroused his sadness for the subjugation of the nation and the change of rulers.

小桃红·采莲女

杨果

满城烟水月微茫，人倚兰舟唱。常记相逢若耶上，隔三湘，碧云望断空惆怅。

美人笑道：莲花相似，情短藕丝长。

采莲人和采莲歌，柳外兰舟过。不管鸳鸯梦惊破。夜如何？有人独上江楼卧。

伤心莫唱，南朝旧曲，司马泪痕多。

采莲湖上棹船回，风约湘裙翠。一曲琵琶数行泪，望君归，芙蓉开尽无消息。

晚凉多少，红鸳白鹭，何处不双飞！

碧湖湖上柳阴阴，人影澄波浸，常记年时对花饮。到如今，西风吹断回文锦。

羡他一对，鸳鸯飞去，残梦蓼花深。

Tune: Red Peach Blossoms · The Lotus Gatherer

Yang Guo

The dimming moon o'er mist-veiled town and water looms. The beauty in orchid boat sings her dream. I oft remember our meeting on silk-washing stream. Now severed by three rivers long, in vain through clouds into the azure sky I gaze. Smiling, the beauty says, "Our hearts are like the lotus blooms: Their root may snap, their fibres join like my song."

Picking lotus, the lotus gatherer is sing. The orchid boat passes by outside the willow trees, regardless of the shattered dreams of the mandarin ducks. How is the night? Someone sleeps alone in the river tower. Don't sing when you're sad, those old songs from the Southern Dynasty, with many tears on Sima's face.

Having gathered the lotus on the lake, she rows. On homeward way, her green skirt ripples when wind blows. A song of pipa brings down tear on tear; In vain she waits for her man to appear. Now lotus blooms all faded, he is not in sight. How many lovebirds red and egrets white.

She sees in the cool evening sky! Nowhere but in pairs will they fly.

The willows on the Bihu Lake are shaded. The shadows of the people are clear and soaked in the waves. I often remember drinking with you by the flowers during the New Year. But now, the west wind brings back no trace of you. Envying those mandarin ducks that fly in pairs, I have only lingering broken dreams.

第一首描写一对青年男女当年邂逅相逢的情景。月色朦胧的夜晚，满城水波一片迷茫，美人在画船上吟唱，回忆当初和男子在水上相逢的美好情景。如今虽然相距咫尺却如同隔着三湘，即使望断天涯也无法相聚。最后三句是女子的回答：虽然相互依恋的时间短暂，但我对你的思念却像藕丝那样绵长。藕断丝连，"丝"与"思"为谐音双关。

The first poem describes the scene when a couple of young people meet in the early years. In a moonlit night, the town is mist-veiled and water looms. The beauty sings in orchid boat, recalling the beautiful scene of meeting the man on the stream. Now, though close in memory, they are three rivers away from each other, and cannot get together even if gazing "through clouds into the azure sky". The last three lines are the woman's response: Although we fell in love with each other not too long ago, my longing for you last as long as lotus fibres. Apparently severed but actually connected, their "思" (si, yearning) is homophonic with "丝" (si, fibres).

第二首写离人的相思之情，以南朝之事抒发哀金之隐痛。前两句用白描的手法写采莲人欢悦的采莲情景。紧接着闻歌垂泪的伤心之景让基调突然转向忧郁。作者担心采莲女唱出南朝旧曲，于是委婉地说出了他心灵的隐痛，惆怅之情溢于言表。

The second poem writes the lovesickness of parted lovers, and the poet's hidden pain for the Jin Dynasty. The first two lines depict the scene of the lotus gatherers working happily. Then suddenly, the tone turns into depression when depicting Sima shedding tears upon hearing the familiar old songs. The author was worried that the lotus gatherers would sing old songs from the Southern Dynasty, so he euphemistically expressed the hidden pain in his heart, which overflowed with melancholy.

第三首描写的是采莲女对远方亲人的思念之深。开篇就刻画了一个风姿绰约的采莲女形象，她触景生情，琵琶、芙蓉、红鹭、白鹭都成为她相思的引子，最后以景寄情，以物喻人，在物我对比、情景交融中升华主题，言尽而意无穷。

The third poem describes the lotus gatherer's longing for her loved one far away. It begins with the depiction of a charming lotus gatherer, who is moved by what she sees. Pipa, lotus blooms, lovebirds red and egrets white, all of which become the trigger of her lovesickness. Finally, by conveying emotions through the scenery and using metaphors to describe people's characteristics, it gets to the theme through the ego-others contrast and a fusion of feelings with the natural setting.

第四首表达了失恋女子的惆怅。前半首回忆当年欢爱的情景，当年越是幸福惬意，现在回忆起来便越是伤心凄楚。后半首写如今物是人非，徒留"残梦"，表现了形单影只的寂寞与愁苦。

The fourth poem expresses the melancholy of a lovelorn woman. The first half recalls the scene of love back then. The happier they were, the sadder she is now. The second half writes that so much has changed now, with nothing left but "lingering broken dreams", expressing the lonely sadness.

此曲语言清丽婉约，由景及人，又由人及景，以湖上美景引出回忆与现况的今昔对比，将物是人非、人去楼空的悲伤表达得尤为贴切，使得曲情愈发凄婉、悲怆。

The language is elegant and graceful in this poem. The beautiful scenery on the lake leads to the contrast between the memory and the present, appropriately expressing the sadness that things have changed and people have gone, making the poem more pathetic.

天净沙·秋思
Sunny Sand · Autumn Thoughts

扫码看视频

作为一位生活在元代的汉人，马致远在追求理想抱负的路上可能注定会是坎坷的。忙碌、漂泊半生，眼看岁之将暮，他却只能依旧漫无目的、风尘仆仆地前行，却不知奔向人生的何处。他骑着一匹消瘦的老马，迎着西风，在荒芜的山脉中踽踽独行，思念着故乡，于是他写下了这首小令。

As a Han Chinese living in the Yuan Dynasty, maybe Ma Zhiyuan's road was destined to be bumpy in the pursuit of his ideals and ambitions. Having a busy and wandering life for half a lifetime, he rode a lean old horse, traveling alone in the desolate mountains against the west wind aimlessly and tiredly, not knowing where to go, though the end of this year was drawing near. Missing his hometown, he wrote this short lyric.

天净沙·秋思
马致远

枯藤老树昏鸦，

小桥流水人家，

古道西风瘦马。

夕阳西下，

断肠人在天涯。

Sunny Sand · Autumn Thoughts
Ma Zhiyuan

Over old trees wreathed with rotten vines fly evening crows;

Under a small bridge near a cottage a stream flows;

On ancient road in the west wind a lean horse goes.

Westward declines the sun;

Far, far from home is the heartbroken one.

《天净沙·秋思》即使在小令中也算是短的了，一共只有五句二十八个字，除题目之外，全曲无一个"秋"，却被后人誉为"秋思之祖"。

"Sunny Sand · Autumn Thoughts" is short even in a short lyric, with a total of only five verses and twenty-eight Chinese characters. Except for the title, there is no "autumn" in the whole poem, but it is praised as "the ancestor of autumn thoughts" by later generations.

正文无一"秋"字，却处处写秋；无一"思"字，却字字含"思"。用极其简洁的文字，描绘出一幅生动的深秋羁旅图，其艺术特色鲜明。

There is no character for "autumn" throughout the text, but autumn is depicted everywhere; there is no character for "thoughts", but "thoughts" are contained in every character. With extremely concise words, it portrays a vivid picture of a traveler in late autumn. Its artistic features are distinct.

首先，以景托情，景中含情。作者选取了"枯藤""老树""昏鸦"等一系列富有深秋特色的意象，营造出一种凄凉、萧瑟的氛围，烘托出游子孤独、愁苦的心情。

First of all, it expresses emotions through scenery, and the emotions are contained within the scenery. The author selected a series of images characteristic of late autumn,

such as "rotten vines", "old trees", and "evening crows", creating a desolate and bleak atmosphere, highlighting the lonely and distressed mood of the traveler.

其次，对比鲜明。"小桥流水人家"的温馨、宁静与"古道西风瘦马"的凄凉形成鲜明对比，更凸显出游子的羁旅之苦和思乡之情。

Secondly, the contrast is distinct. The warm and peaceful "Under a small bridge near a cottage a stream flows" forms a strong contrast with the desolation of "On ancient road in the west wind a lean horse goes", further highlighting the traveler's hardships and homesickness during the journey.

山坡羊·潼关怀古
Tune: Sheep on the Slope ·
Thinking of the Past on My Way to Tong Pass

扫码看视频

《山坡羊·潼关怀古》是元曲作家张养浩的散曲代表作。天历二年（1329 年），因关中旱灾，张养浩被任命为陕西行台中丞以赈灾民，亲睹人民的深重灾难，不禁感慨、叹喟，遂散尽家财，尽心尽力去救灾，终因过分操劳而殉职。这首散曲就写在他应召前往关中的途中。

"Tune: Sheep on the Slope · Thinking of the Past on My Way to Tong Pass" is a representative piece of Zhang Yanghao, a Yuan Dynasty playwright. In the second year of the Tianli era (1329 CE), Zhang Yanghao was appointed as the Deputy Officer of Shaanxi Province to provide disaster relief to the people affected by severe drought in Guanzhong (the Weihe River area in Shaanxi Province). Witnessing the profound suffering of the people, he felt deeply moved and spent all his wealth and energy to help them overcome the disaster. Unfortunately, due to excessive workload, he passed away while fulfilling his duties. This piece of Yuan opera was written on his way to Guanzhong.

山坡羊·潼关怀古

张养浩

峰峦如聚，波涛如怒，山河表里潼关路。

望西都，意踌躇。

伤心秦汉经行处，宫阙万间都做了土。

兴，百姓苦；亡，百姓苦。

Tune: Sheep on the Slope ·
Thinking of the Past on My Way to Tong Pass

Zhang Yanghao

Peaks like brows knit,

Angry waves spit.

With mountain and river far and near,

On the road to Tong Pass I appear.

Gazing on Western Capital,

I hesitate, alas!

To see the place where ancient warriors did pass

The ancient palaces, hall on hall,

Are turned to dust, one and all.

Before my eyes,

The empire's rise

Is people's woe;

The empire's fall

Is also people's woe.

全曲第一层写潼关雄伟险要的形势，一个"聚"字表现了峰峦的数量众多和峰峦的动感，一个"怒"字写出了波涛的汹涌澎湃，"山河表里潼关路"之感便油然而生。第二层，作者从潼关西望旧朝故都长安，抚今追昔，思绪万千，感慨横生。王朝兴，民为"宫阙万间"而劳役；政权更迭，战火连连，百姓流离失所，而那些宫殿，最终都变作了土。第三层从描绘雄阔的山河气象，到沉痛的怀古之叹，由王朝兴衰更迭想

到百姓流离失所——"兴，百姓苦；亡，百姓苦"。

The first section of the entire piece portrays the majestic and perilous situation of Tong Pass. The word "聚" (gather) represents the large number and dynamism of the peaks, while the word "怒" (angry) depicts the surging and turbulent waves. Hence the feeling of "With mountain and river far and near, on the road to Tong Pass I appear". In the second section, the author gazes westward from Tong Pass towards the old capital of Chang'an, reminiscing about the past and reflecting on a myriad of thoughts. When the empire rises, people are forced to work for "the ancient palaces, hall on hall", but when regime changes and wars continue, people are displaced, and those palaces are turned to dust in the end. The third section transitions from depicting the majestic and awe-inspiring scenery of mountains and rivers to a somber lamentation of the past, and it also reflects on the rise and fall of dynasties and the displacement of the people—"The empire's rise is people's woe; the empire's fall is also people's woe."

全曲层层深入，由写景而怀古，再引发议论，完美融合了苍茫的景色、深沉的情感和精辟的议论，字里行间都充满了对百姓的深切同情和关怀，饱含对历代王朝深深的遗恨和对元朝统治的深刻批判，其忧国忧民的感情感人至深，令人心生敬意。

The entire piece delves deeper layer by layer, transitioning from scenic descriptions to reminiscing about the past and sparking discussions. It perfectly combines vast landscapes, profound emotions, and insightful commentary. The lines are filled with heartfelt compassion and carefulness for the people, along with the great regret of past dynasties and profound criticism on Yuan Dynasty's rule. The author's profound patriotic and humanitarian sentiments are deeply moving and deserve people's respect.

再别康桥

Saying Goodbye to Cambridge Again

扫码看视频

《再别康桥》是现代诗人徐志摩最著名的诗篇之一，抒发了他故地重游时对康桥依依惜别的深情。在剑桥留学的两年里，诗人深受西方教育的熏陶及欧美浪漫主义和唯美派诗人的影响，追求个性解放，追求"爱、自由、美"，但回国后理想与现实的落差，使曾经似"快乐的雪花"般的诗人变成了"卑微"的"残苇"，理想的幻灭激起诗人对往昔康桥岁月的回忆。全诗以离别康桥时的情感起伏为线索，诗人将自己的生活体验化作缕缕情思，融汇在笔下康桥美丽的景色里，反映了诗人复杂的情感——有对康桥的爱恋，有对往昔生活的追忆，有对理想幻灭的感伤，有对离愁的无可奈何。全诗以三个"轻轻的"起笔，将至深的情怀幻化为"西天的云彩"，用虚实相间的手法，描绘了一幅幅流动的画面，构成了一处处美妙的意境。

"Saying Goodbye to Cambridge Again" is one of the most famous poems by the modern poet Xu Zhimo, expressing his deep affection for Cambridge when revisiting Cambridge and reluctantly bidding farewell. During his two years of study in Cambridge University, Xu was deeply influenced by Western education, as well as the romantic and aesthetic poems written by European and American poets, and began to pursue personal liberation and the ideals of "love, freedom, and beauty". However, upon returning to his homeland, the gap between ideal and reality made the poet—once like "joyful snowflakes", turned into a "humble withered reed" as his ideals were shattered. The experience stirred up his memories of past days in Cambridge. The whole poem revolves around Xu's fluctuating emotions after leaving Cambridge. He transformed his life experiences into repetitive sentiments, blending them into the beautiful scenery of Cambridge where his complex emotions were reflected—from his love for Cambridge, yearning for his past life, lamentation over shattered ideals, to helplessness in the face of separation. The poem begins with the word "quietly" three times, turning deep emotions into "clouds in the western sky". Through a combination of reality and illusion, Xu depicted flowing pictures, creating a series of beautiful artistic conceptions.

再 别 康 桥

徐志摩

轻轻的我走了，

正如我轻轻的来；

我轻轻的招手，

作别西天的云彩。

那河畔的金柳，

是夕阳中的新娘；

波光里的艳影，

在我的心头荡漾。

软泥上的青荇，

油油的在水底招摇；

在康河的柔波里，

我甘心做一条水草!

那榆荫下的一潭,
不是清泉,是天上虹;
揉碎在浮藻间,
沉淀着彩虹似的梦。

寻梦?撑一支长篙,
向青草更青处漫溯;
满载一船星辉,
在星辉斑斓里放歌。

但我不能放歌,
悄悄是别离的笙箫;
夏虫也为我沉默,
沉默是今晚的康桥!

悄悄的我走了,
正如我悄悄的来;
我挥一挥衣袖,
不带走一片云彩。

Saying Goodbye to Cambridge Again

Xu Zhimo

Very quietly I take my leave

As quietly as I came here

Quietly I wave good-bye

To the rosy clouds in the western sky

The golden willows by the riverside

Are young brides in the setting sun

Their reflections on the shimmering waves

Always linger in the depth of my heart

The floating heart growing in the sludge

Sways leisurely under the water

In the gentle waves of Cambridge

I would be a water plant

That pool under the shade of elm trees

Holds not water but the rainbow from the sky

Shattered to pieces among the duckweeds

Is the sediment of a rainbow-like dream

To seek a dream? Just to pole a boat upstream

To where the green grass is more verdant

Or to have the boat fully loaded with starlight

And sing aloud in the splendour of starlight

But I cannot sing aloud

Quietness is my farewell music

Even summer insects help silence for me

Silent is Cambridge tonight

Very quietly I take my leave

As quietly as I came here

Gently I flick my sleeves

Not even a wisp of cloud will I bring away

在清华大学教授蓝棣之看来，"不带走一片云彩"，一方面是说诗人的洒脱，他不是见到美好的东西就要据为己有的人；另一方面是说一片云彩也不要带走，让康桥这个魂牵梦绕的感情世界以最完整的面貌保存下来，让昔日的梦、昔日的感情完好无缺。

Lan Dizhi, a professor at Tsinghua University explains the line—"Not even a wisp of cloud will I bring away". On the one hand, it signifies that the poet is not a person who takes possession of beautiful things he sees. On the other hand, it means that he doesn't take away a single cloud, allowing Cambridge, the place that is so intertwined with the poet's dreams, to be preserved in its most complete form and to keep the past dreams and emotions intact.

全诗结构形式严谨整齐，错落有致，共7节，每节4行，组成两个平行台阶；第1、3行稍短，第2、4行稍长，每行6至8字不等，诗人似乎有意把格律诗与自由诗这两种形式糅合起来，使之成为一种新的诗歌形式。诗的语言清新秀丽，节奏轻柔委婉、和谐自然，伴随着情感的起伏跳跃，犹如一曲悦耳徐缓的散板，轻盈婉转，拨动着读者的心弦。

The poem is structured in a precise and neat manner, with seven stanzas, each consisting of four lines and forming two "parallel steps". The first and third lines are shorter, while the second and fourth lines are longer, with each line containing six to eight characters. The poet seems to intentionally blend the forms of regulated verse with free verse, creating a new form of poetry. The language is fresh and beautiful, with a gentle and graceful rhythm that flows harmoniously and naturally. Along with the ups and downs of emotions, it flows like a mellifluous and slow-paced rhythm, light and elegant, touching the reader's heartstrings.

这首诗将具体景物与想象糅合在一起，巧妙地把气氛、感情、景象融汇为意境，于动静相衬中见深情美，于虚实结合间见离情美，于比拟夸张里见浓情美，景中有情，情中有景。诗人后来曾满怀深情地说："我的眼是康桥教我睁的，我的求知欲是康桥给我拨动的，我的自我意识是康桥给我胚胎的。"

This poem skillfully blends specific scenery with imagination, ingeniously merging atmosphere, emotions, and imagery into a poetic realm. Through the contrast of movement and stillness, it reveals profound beauty in sentimental moments. Through the combination of reality and imagination, it captures the beauty of distance and separation. Through the use of metaphors and exaggeration, it depicts the intense beauty of emotions. The scenery is within emotions and emotions are within scenery. The poet later said passionately, "Cambridge opened my eyes, stirred my thirst for knowledge, and nurtured my self-awareness."

沁园春·汉字颂
Spring in Soothing Park · Ode to Characters

扫码看视频

汉字被誉为"中华文化的基石"，具有独特的符号性、文化内涵和艺术魅力，在世界范围内受到了广泛欣赏与关注。赵安民从事诗词、书法、国学创作与研究多年，他的这首词以画的风韵入词，内含两汉辞赋之风，展现汉字的波澜壮阔之美。

Chinese characters, known as the "cornerstone of Chinese culture", have received wide appreciation and attention worldwide due to their unique symbolic, cultural and artistic charm. Zhao Anmin has been engaged in the creation and research of poetry, calligraphy, and traditional Chinese studies for years. His lyrics starts with paintings, embodying the charm of the Northern and Southern Han dynasties' literary compositions, and demonstrating the grandeur and magnificence of Chinese characters.

沁园春·汉字颂
赵安民

故国东方，汉字通神，文脉久昌。

幸羲皇创卦，天开一画；颉臣造字，界破洪荒。

独体方圆，单音扬抑，义见形声万物彰。

抒情志，有重章叠唱，思幻言长。

今朝岁月铿锵，引无数诗人赋慨慷。

看嘤鸣汉语，亲和世界；龙飞书法，流美诗乡。

事在人为，梦由心画，丝路驼铃乐万邦。

挥毫也，得江山助兴，绘我新章。

Spring in Soothing Park · Ode to Characters

Zhao Anmin

East Clime, my motherland!

Chinese characters grand,

Letters we all command.

Hexagrams Lord Hsi did create,

A Heavenly stroke great;

Cangjie first words designed,

Hence no barriers to find.

Lo, shaped square and round;

Hark, the melodious sound!

Meaning and form reveal

all without bound.

Expressed our wills strong,

Chapters and refrains make the song;

Thought's profound and speech long.

We have the best era today;

Countless poets loudly

and proudly sing their lay.

Chinese is chirped to you and me;

This world so endeared be;

Calligraphy seems live;

Muses with grace arrive.

One can well play his part,

A dream is from the heart,

All nations on the Silk Road

their trek start.

My writing brush I wave.

Mountains, rivers add to my zest,

I draw a chapter blessed.

词的上阕赞美了汉字的独特和博大精深之处。开篇"故国东方"气势恢宏，接着强调了汉字源远流长的文化底蕴，并以磅礴的手笔描写汉字的创造过程与神奇之处，描绘了汉字的特点以及汉字的字形和音律，写出了汉字的语言美和文化价值，反映了作者对中华文化的热爱和推崇。

The first part of this lyric praises the uniqueness and profoundness of Chinese characters. It starts with the grand atmosphere of "East Clime, my motherland!" and emphasizes the long-standing cultural heritage of Chinese characters. It magnificently presents the creation and wonders of Chinese characters, highlighting their characteristics, form and phonetic rhythm. It emphasizes the linguistic beauty and cultural significance of Chinese characters, conveying the author's profound affection and reverence for Chinese culture.

词的下阕强调汉字随着时代的变迁依旧熠熠生辉，不仅为中国人所熟知，也为世界所共享。作者以"今朝岁月铿锵"为起点，提到了汉字已经成为中华文化的象征，也提到了汉字书法和诗词之美，最后借助丝路与驼铃的意象，强调了汉字、书法与文化间的交流和融合，写出了作者内心的追求，寄寓着对于我国未来的美好向往与期盼。

The second part emphasizes that Chinese characters still shine with their own charm despite the change of times. They are not only familiar to Chinese people but also shared worldwide. Beginning with "We have the best era today", the poet mentions how Chinese characters have evolved into symbols of Chinese culture. The lyric also praises the artistry of Chinese calligraphy and poetry, and emphasizes the exchange and integration between Chinese characters, calligraphy, and culture, with the imagery of the Silk Road and camel bells. The poet's inner pursuit and hope for China's future are both embodied in the lyric.

整首词语言简练，寓意深远，表达了作者对汉字的热爱和赞扬，传递着一种信念和力量，向世界展现了汉字的魅力。

The entire lyric is concise in language, and profound in meaning, expressing the poet's affection and praise for Chinese characters. In addition, it conveys faith and strength, and showcases the charm of Chinese characters to the world.

节日里的中国

China in Festivals

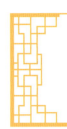

导 语
Introduction

中国是一个历史文化悠久的国家，节日文化是中华文化中非常重要的组成部分。传统节日有着丰富多彩的庆祝方式和习俗，与中国人的生产生活密不可分，是凝聚中国人智慧、维系中国人情感的纽带，是中华文化传承和发展的重要载体，也是国家极为宝贵的非物质文化遗产。中国传统节日承载着中华民族丰富的文化内涵和历史底蕴，反映了中华民族的智慧和创造力，不仅是中华文化的瑰宝，也是全人类共同的文化遗产。

China is a country with a long history and rich culture. Festival culture is an important part of Chinese culture. Traditional festivals have diverse celebrations and customs, and are closely related to the production and life of the Chinese people. They serve as the bonds that unite Chinese people's wisdom and emotions, important carriers of the inheritance and development of Chinese culture, and also invaluable intangible cultural heritage of the country. Traditional Chinese festivals carry the rich cultural connotations and historical legacy of the Chinese nation. They showcase the wisdom and creativity of the Chinese nation, and are not only treasures of Chinese culture but also share cultural heritage of all mankind.

中国传统节日蕴含着特定的文化意义和价值观，反映了中华民族的历史、文化传统和社会习俗。人们通过各种活动和仪式庆祝传统节日，传承和弘扬中华文化，增强民族自豪感和凝聚力。传统节日承载着多个历史时期的经验和故事，比如春秋时期，晋文公为纪念介子推，将放火烧绵山的这一天定为寒食节；人们在端午节赛龙舟、佩香囊、吃粽子以表达对诗人屈原的怀念和敬意。传统节日承载着独特的文化意义和价值观，如中华民族最重要的传统节日——春节，它不仅是新年的开始，也是家庭团圆、

亲情友爱、敬老爱幼等中华传统美德的体现。春节期间，人们会进行贴春联、挂灯笼、放鞭炮、赏烟花、舞龙舞狮等活动，意在祈求吉祥、庆贺新年，也蕴含着驱邪避灾、团团圆圆和家庭和睦的愿望。人们在重阳节用敬祖、尊老、敬老等行为体现孝道思亲和慎终追远等中华民族的优良传统。

Traditional Chinese festivals embody specific cultural meanings and values, reflecting the history, cultural traditions, and social customs of the Chinese nation. Through various activities and ceremonies, people celebrate traditional festivals to inherit and promote Chinese culture, enhancing national pride and cohesion. Traditional festivals carry the experience and stories of multiple historical periods. For example, during the Spring and Autumn Period, Duke Wen of Jin established the Cold Food Festival to commemorate Jie Zitui, who had made great sacrifice to save his Lord. Moreover, during the Dragon Boat Festival, by participating in dragon boat races, wearing fragrant sachets, and eating zongzi, people express their nostalgia and respect for the poet Qu Yuan. Traditional festivals carry unique cultural meanings and values. For example, the most important traditional festival for the Chinese people is the Spring Festival, which not only marks the beginning of the new year but also embodies the traditional Chinese virtues of family reunion, filial piety, and love for one's elders and children. During the Spring Festival, people engage in activities such as pasting couplets, hanging lanterns, setting off firecrackers, watching fireworks, and performing dragon and lion dances. These activities are meant to pray for good fortune, celebrate the new year, and symbolize the desire to ward off evil, reunite with family, and maintain harmonious relationships at home. During the Double Ninth Festival, people demonstrate filial piety and respect for the elderly, embodying the Chinese tradition of honoring ancestors, respecting and caring for one's elders, and commemorating the departed.

中国传统节日在庆祝活动、习俗和艺术表现等方面具有独特的审美意蕴，反映了中华民族对自然、社会和生活的独特感悟和审美追求。传统节日的庆祝活动往往具有很强的视觉和听觉冲击力，如春节的烟花、鞭炮、舞龙舞狮，元宵节的花灯，中元节的河灯，等等，它们同时又具有很高的审美价值。传统节日的习俗往往蕴含着人们对美好生活的向往和对自然规律的尊重。例如，春节期间的春联、年画、窗花等装饰艺术，端午节的粽子、中秋节的月饼等食品制作，都体现了精湛的手工艺和独特的审美风格。传统节日中使用的各种文化符号，如春节的红色、端午节的艾叶、中秋节的圆月等，都具有丰富的象征意义和审美价值。这些符号不仅反映了人们对自然和社会的认知，也表达了人们对美好生活的追求。传统节日中的戏曲、舞蹈、音乐、诗词等艺

术形式也体现了中华民族的艺术创造力和高尚的审美情趣。

Traditional Chinese festivals have unique aesthetic connotations in terms of celebration activities, customs, and artistic expressions, reflecting the unique perception and aesthetic pursuit of the Chinese nation towards nature, society, and life. The celebration activities of traditional festivals often possess strong visual and auditory impacts, such as the fireworks, firecrackers, dragon and lion dances during the Spring Festival, the lanterns during the Lantern Festival, and the river lanterns during the Zhongyuan Festival, all of which have high aesthetic value. The customs of traditional festivals often embody people's yearning for a better life and respect for natural laws. For example, the decorative arts such as the Spring Festival couplets, New Year's paintings, and window flowers, as well as the food preparations for Dragon Boat Festival's zongzi and Mid-Autumn Festival's mooncakes, all reflect exquisite handicrafts and unique aesthetic styles. The various cultural symbols used in traditional festivals, such as the red color of the Spring Festival, the mugwort leaves of the Dragon Boat Festival, and the full moon of the Mid-Autumn Festival, all have rich symbolic meanings and aesthetic values. These symbols not only reflect people's understanding of nature and society but also express their pursuit of a better life. The traditional festivals' art forms, such as opera, dance, music and poetry, also embody the artistic creativity and noble aesthetic taste of the Chinese nation.

中国传统节日是各族人民共同的文化记忆和身份认同，激发了人们对中国传统文化的热爱。庆祝节日的活动将人们聚集在一起，共同享受节日的喜庆和欢乐，使人们更加团结和亲近，有助于维系社会的稳定和和谐。让我们一起来学习和欣赏中国传统节日，感受中华民族的智慧和创造力，体验独特而深刻的审美文化，更好地传承和弘扬中华文化，增强民族自豪感和凝聚力。

Traditional Chinese festivals are a shared cultural memory and identity for all ethnic groups, inspiring people's love for traditional Chinese culture. The celebrations bring people together to enjoy the joy and happiness of the festivities, fostering unity and closeness among people and contributing to social stability and harmony. Let us learn about and appreciate traditional Chinese festivals together, experience the wisdom and creativity of the Chinese nation, and enjoy a unique and profound aesthetic culture. This will help better inherit and promote Chinese culture as well as enhance national pride and cohesion.

春 节
The Spring Festival

扫码看视频

春节指农历新年，俗称"年节"，是中华民族最隆重的传统佳节。

The Spring Festival, commonly known as the Chinese New Year, is the traditional lunar New Year, and it is the most solemn traditional festival of the Chinese nation.

节日起源
Festival Origin

据记载，中华民族过春节已有四千多年的历史。关于春节的起源有很多说法。民间一种有趣的说法是一个叫"年"的凶猛怪兽，每到腊月三十，便窜村挨户觅食人肉，残害生灵。有一个腊月三十的晚上，"年"窜到村庄，被牧童比赛时用的牛鞭子的啪啪声、一家门口晒着的大红衣裳和一户人家辉煌的灯火吓得夹着尾巴溜了。人们由此摸准了"年"有怕响、怕红、怕光的弱点，便想到许多抵御它的方法，如贴红对联、燃放爆竹等，这些方法逐渐演化成春节的风俗。

According to records, the Chinese nation has celebrated the Spring Festival for more than 4,000 years. There are many folk takes about the origin of the Spring Festival. An interesting folk tale is that in ancient times, there was a ferocious monster called "Nian", which rampaged through villages on the 30th of the 12th lunar month, preying on people

and livestock. Once, on the evening of the 30th day of the lunar month, "Nian" rushed to the village again, but was frightened by the sound of shepherd boys' whip used in a competition, the bright red clothes drying at the door of a house, and the brilliant lights of a household, thus fled with his tail between legs. People discovered that "Nian" was afraid of loud noises, the color red, and bright lights, so they came up with various ways to defend against it, such as pasting red couplets and setting off firecrackers, which gradually evolved into the customs of the Spring Festival.

节日习俗
Festival Customs

扫尘是春节的传统习俗，有"除尘布新"的含义。每逢春节来临，家家户户都会将室内外彻底打扫干净，将衣、被、用具洗刷一新，干干净净地迎新春。

Sweeping the dust is a traditional custom of the Spring Festival, which means "getting rid of the old and ushering in the new". When the Spring Festival approaches, every household will thoroughly clean their indoor and outdoor areas, wash their clothes, quilt covers and bed sheets, and utensils, and welcome the new year with a fresh and clean start.

贴春联和"福"字也是由来已久的春节习俗。春联以工整、对偶、简洁、精巧的文字描绘时代背景，表达美好愿望。"福"字指福气、福运，体现了人们对幸福生活的向往。

Pasting the Spring Festival couplets and the Chinese character "fu" (meaning "blessing" or "happiness") is also a long-standing custom during the Spring Festival. The Spring Festival couplets depict the background of the times and express beautiful wishes with neat, antithetical, concise, and exquisite writing. The character "fu" refers to blessing, good fortune and people's longing for a happy life.

春节还有守岁的风俗。除夕夜，全家团聚在一起，吃过年夜饭后就围坐在一起闲聊，等着辞旧迎新的时刻。

Staying up late on New Year's Eve is also a tradition. On New Year's Eve, the whole family reunite for dinner and sit together and chat, waiting for the moment to bid farewell to the old year and usher in a new year.

燃放爆竹是自汉代起就有的春节习俗。中国民间自古就有"开门爆竹"一说，家家户户在新年开门的第一件事就是燃放爆竹，"爆竹声中一岁除，春风送暖入屠苏"。

Setting off firecrackers have been a custom in the Spring Festival since the Han Dynasty. Since ancient times, there has been a saying in Chinese folklore that "everyone sets off firecrackers as soon as they open the door for the start of the new year". Therefore, many households would take it as the first thing to do outside in the New Year. "With the sound of firecrackers, the old year is gone, and the warm spring wind enters the house."

拜年也是春节的传统习俗。大年初一，人们早起走亲访友，登门拜年，互致问候。春节拜年时，长辈会给晚辈压岁钱，据说压岁钱可以压住邪祟，晚辈得到压岁钱就可以平平安安度过一岁。

Paying New Year greetings. On the first day of the Lunar New Year, people wake up early to visit relatives and friends and exchange greetings. During the visits, elders will give red envelopes to younger generations. It is said that red envelopes can suppress evil spirits, and younger generations can spend the year safely by receiving red envelopes.

春节是浓浓的情意、深深的祝福、绵绵的怀念、切切的问候，春节的习俗更是几千年来流传下来的中国人民的生命追求和情感寄托。

The Spring Festival is full of affection, blessing, nostalgia, and greetings. The customs of the Spring Festival have been passed down for thousands of years as the pursuit of life and emotional sustenance of the Chinese people.

节日饮食
Festival Diet

饺子是年夜饭桌上必不可少的美食。饺子的形状像元宝，包饺子意味着包住福运，吃饺子带有"招财进宝"的吉祥含义。

Dumplings. Dumplings are an essential delicacy on the New Year's Eve dinner table. Dumplings are shaped like gold ingots. Making dumplings means wrapping up good luck, and eating dumplings carries the auspicious meaning of "bringing in wealth and treasures".

年糕谐音"年高"，春节吃年糕的寓意为万事如意、年年高。黄色、白色年糕象征着黄金、白银，寓意为新年发财。

Niangao. The homophonic pronunciation of "niangao" in Chinese sounds similar to "getting higher year by year". Eating niangao (New Year's Cake, made of glutinous rice flour) during the Spring Festival implies wishing for everything to go smoothly and be prosperous year after year. The yellow and white colors of the New Year's cakes symbolize gold and silver, representing the wish for wealth in the New Year.

元宵，南方叫作"汤圆"，在江苏、上海等地，大年初一早晨都有吃汤圆的习俗，该习俗象征一家人团团圆圆、和和美美。

Yuanxiao. In southern China, it is called "tangyuan" (glue puddings, made of glutinous rice flour). In Jiangsu, Shanghai and other places, it is customary to eat glue puddings on the morning of the first day of the New Year, symbolizing the reunion and harmony of the family.

春节是中华优秀传统文化的重要载体，蕴含着中华文化的智慧和结晶，凝聚着中国人的生命追求和情感寄托，传承着中国人的社会伦理观念。据不完全统计，受中华文化的影响，已有近20个国家和地区把中国春节定为法定节假日。2023年12月22日，第78届联合国大会协商一致通过决议，将春节（农历新年）确定为联合国假日。春节已走出中国，走向世界。

The Spring Festival is an important carrier of fine traditional Chinese culture, crystallizing the Chinese wisdom and cultural essence, reflecting the pursuit of life and emotional sustenance of the Chinese people, and inheriting the social and ethical concepts of the Chinese people. According to incomplete statistics, influenced by Chinese culture, nearly 20 countries and regions have designated the Spring Festival as a legal holiday. On December 22, 2023, the 78th session of the United Nations General Assembly unanimously passed a resolution designating the Spring Festival (Lunar New Year) as a United Nations holiday. It can be said that the Spring Festival has now gone out of China and into the world.

扫码看视频

元 宵 节
The Lantern Festival

"正月十五到，欢乐闹元宵。"每年农历的正月十五，就会迎来中国的传统节日——元宵节。

"On the fifteenth day of the first lunar month, we celebrate the Lantern Festival happily." The traditional Lantern Festival falls on the fifteenth day of the first lunar month every year.

节日起源
Festival Origin

元宵节是中国的传统节日，早在两千多年前就已经成为一个具有重要意义的节日。正月是农历的元月，古人称"夜"为"宵"，正月十五之夜是一年中第一个月圆之夜，也是一元复始、大地回春的夜晚，所以正月十五称为"元宵节"，又称"上元节""灯节"。据有关资料与民俗传说记载，正月十五这一天在西汉已受到重视。汉文帝下令将正月十五定为元宵节。南北朝时，元宵张灯渐成民俗风气。唐朝时，中外文化交流往来密切，佛教大兴，官员、百姓普遍在正月十五这一天"燃灯供佛"，于是佛家灯火遍布民间，此后元宵张灯成为法定之事。

The Lantern Festival is a traditional festival in China that has been of great significance for more than 2,000 years. The first lunar month is also called the "Yuan month". Since "night" was called "Xiao" by the ancients, the night on the fifteenth day of the first lunar month, which is the first night of a year to see a full moon, and also a time when a new year begins and spring returns to the earth, is therefore called "the Lantern Festival" or "Shangyuan Festival". According to the records and folklore, people in Western Han Dynasty have took the fifteenth day of the first lunar month very seriously. Emperor Wen of Han designated the day as the Lantern Festival. During the Northern and Southern Dynasties, lighting lanterns during the Lantern Festival gradually became a custom. In the Tang Dynasty, there were close cultural exchanges between China and foreign countries, and Buddhism flourished. Government officials and ordinary people generally "lit lanterns to worship Buddha" on this day, so the Buddhist lights spread among the people. Since then, the custom of lighting lanterns has become a statutory thing.

节日习俗
Festival Customs

元宵节又称"灯节"，这"灯"便是形态万千、多姿多彩的灯笼。在正月十五到来前，大街小巷都挂满灯笼，有宫灯、兽头灯、走马灯、花卉灯、鸟禽灯等，龙骨轻扎、绢布围蒙、勾线绘彩、燃烛点蜡，每一步都是工匠们的慧心独运，更不用说文人们寄予其间的款款深情。点上一盏彩灯，点亮一盏心灯，祛除黑暗，驱除烦恼，照亮未来。

As its name suggests, the Lantern Festival features a variety of colorful lanterns in various forms. Before the arrival of the fifteenth day of the first lunar month, the streets and alleys are decorated with lanterns, including palace lanterns, animal head lanterns, trotting horse lanterns, flower lanterns, bird lanterns and so on. Tying lantern keels, covering silk cloth, drawing and painting, lighting candles, each of these steps exhibits the feat of the craftsmen. The lanterns light up not only the sky, but also the heart and soul, dispel darkness and troubles and illuminate the future.

猜灯谜又称打灯谜，是从古代就开始流传的元宵节特色活动。灯谜是贴在元宵节花灯上供游人猜的谜语。因猜灯谜能够启迪智慧，且参与的人众多，故逐渐成为元宵节的特色活动流传下来。

Guessing lantern riddles, or playing lantern riddles, is a characteristic activity of the Lantern Festival that has spread since ancient times. Lantern riddles are riddles posted

on lanterns for visitors to guess. Guessing lantern riddles not only inspires wisdom, but also adds to the festive atmosphere. Since there are many people involved, it has gradually become a characteristic activity of the Lantern Festival.

节日饮食
Festival Diet

北方"滚"元宵，南方"包"汤圆，这种圆圆的食物是元宵佳节的特色，以白糖、玫瑰、芝麻、豆沙、核桃仁、果仁、枣泥等为馅，用糯米粉包成圆形，可荤可素，风味各异，可汤煮、油炸、蒸食。无论是元宵，还是汤圆，都寄寓着人们对未来的真诚期待，以及对合家团圆的美好祝愿。

In northern China, people "roll" yuanxiao, while in the south, people "make" tangyuan. The round-shaped food is the characteristic of the Lantern Festival, with sugar, rose, sesame, bean paste, walnut kernels, nuts, jujube paste and so on as fillings, rolled or wrapped into round balls with glutinous rice flour. With different flavors, meat or vegetarian, it can be boiled, fried or steamed. No matter what it is called, yuanxiao or tangyuan, both of them convey people's sincere expectations for the future and good wishes for family reunion.

结尾
Ending

元宵节习俗既具有普遍性，又体现地域性。例如，元宵节的九曲黄河阵灯俗、泉州闹元宵习俗、闽台东石灯俗等已被列入国务院公布的第二批国家级非物质文化遗产名录。近年来，在元宵节到来之际，中国传统文化体验和交流活动在多国举行，海外民众在活动中感受到中国传统文化的巨大魅力。

The Lantern Festival customs are both universal and regional. The Jiuqu Yellow River Lights Array (a kind of folk entertainment which twists and turns like the Yellow River), Quanzhou Lantern Festival custom, Dongshi Lantern Festival custom (celebration in two villages that shared the same name Dongshi in Fujian and Taiwan), etc. are all included in the second batch of national intangible cultural heritage list. In recent years, on the occasion of the Lantern Festival, traditional Chinese culture experience and exchange activities have been held in many countries, from which overseas people can feel the great charm of traditional Chinese culture.

龙 抬 头

The Dragon Heads-Raising Festival

扫码看视频

龙抬头，又被称为"春耕节""农事节""春龙节"，是中国民间传统节日。因节期在农历二月初二，所以也叫"二月二"。

"The Dragon Heads-raising Day", also known as the "Spring Plowing Festival", "Agriculture Festival", and "Spring Dragon Festival", is a traditional Chinese festival. It falls on the second day of the second lunar month, hence its name "Er Yue Er (the Double Second Festival)".

节日起源
Festival Origin

传说龙抬头源于伏羲氏时期。伏羲氏"重农桑，务耕田"，每年二月二这天，"皇娘送饭，御驾亲耕"，自理一亩三分地。后来黄帝、唐尧、虞舜、夏禹纷纷效法先王。到周武王时，他不仅沿袭了这一传统做法，而且将其作为一项国策来实行，在二月初二举行重大仪式，让文武百官亲耕一亩三分地，这便是龙抬头节的历史传说。古人非常重视春雨，二月初二庆祝龙抬头，以示敬龙祈雨，让上天保佑丰收。

Legend has it that the Dragon Heads-raising Festival originated from the period of Fuxi. Fuxi was devoted to agriculture and every year on February 2nd, the Empress would bring food and the Emperor would personally plow a plot of land. Later, this practice was followed by Yellow Emperor, Tang Yao, Yu Shun, and Xia Yu. During the reign of King Wu of Zhou, this tradition was not only continued, but also was adopted as a national policy. On February 2nd, a major ceremony would be held, with civil and military officials cultivating their own parts of land, which becomes the historical legend of the Dragon Heads-raising Festival. In ancient times, people attached great importance to spring rain. Celebrating the Dragon Heads-raising Festival on February 2nd was a way to show respect to the dragon and pray for rain, hoping that heaven would bless a bountiful harvest.

节日习俗
Festival Customs

社祭。相传农历二月初二是土地公公的生日，也称"土地诞"或"社日节"，有的地方家家凑钱为土地神庆祝生日，到土地庙烧香祭祀土地神，敲锣鼓，放鞭炮。

Sacrifice to the Lord of Land. According to legend, Dragon Heads-raising Day is the birthday of the Lord of Land, also known as "Earth God's Birth". In some places, families gather money to celebrate the birthday of the Lord of Land. They visit the Earth God's temple, burn incense, offer sacrifices to the Earth God, play gongs and drums, and set off firecrackers.

剃龙头。二月二这一天，大人、孩子都剃头，叫"剃喜头"。特别是男孩子，要"剃龙头"，据说在这一天理发能够带来一年的好运，寓意为红运当头。

Dragon heads shaving. On the Dragon Heads-raising Festival, both adults and children cut their hair, known as "shaving the auspicious head". Boys get their hair cut in a style called "Dragon Head Shaving", because it is said that getting a haircut, also known as "Cutting Hair of Dragons" on this day can bring good fortune for a year, symbolizing auspiciousness.

炒玉米。相传玉龙为解人间干旱之苦而降雨，被玉帝囚禁，玉帝规定金豆开花方能释放玉龙。人们为救玉龙一起炒玉米，炒过的玉米看起来像"金豆开花"，于是玉龙被释放。这一传说流传到今天。现在有的地方人们会在这一天爆玉米花。

Frying corn. Legend has it that Jade Dragon brought rain to relieve the drought in the human world but was imprisoned by the Jade Emperor, who decreed that only when gold beans blossomed, could Jade Dragon be released. People fried corn together to save Jade Dragon, which looked like "gold beans blossoming", and the Jade Dragon was set free. This legend has been passed down to this day. Now in some places, people pop corn on this day.

节日饮食
Festival Diet

吃"龙"食。二月二这一天的饮食多以龙为名，吃水饺叫"吃龙耳"，吃春饼叫"吃龙鳞"，吃米饭叫"吃龙子"，吃面条叫"食龙须"，吃馄饨叫"吃龙眼"，面条、馄饨一起煮叫作"龙拿珠"，吃猪头称作"食龙头"，吃葱饼叫作"撕龙皮"。

Eating "Dragon" food. The food on the Dragon Head-raising Festival is mostly named after dragon. Eating dumplings is called "Eating Dragon's Ears"; eating spring pancakes is

174

"Eating Dragon's Scales"; eating rice is "Eating Dragon's Offspring"; eating noodles, "Eating Dragon's Whiskers"; eating wontons, "Eating Dragon's Eyes"; cooking noodles and wontons together is called "Loong Na Zhu", which means that dragon holds the pearl; eating pig's head, "Eating Dragon's Head", and eating scallion pancakes, "Tearing Dragon's Skin".

二月二龙抬头围绕美好的龙神信仰而展开，寄托着人们祈龙赐福，期待风调雨顺、五谷丰登的强烈愿望。随着时代的变迁，其节日内容越来越丰富。

The Dragon Heads-raising Festival on the second day of the second lunar month revolves around the belief in the auspicious dragon deity, symbolizing people's strong wishes for blessing, good weather, and a bountiful harvest. With the development of society and the passage of time, the festival has become more diverse and enriched in content.

端 午 节
The Dragon Boat Festival

扫码看视频

农历五月初五是中国的传统节日端午节，是中华民族古老的传统节日之一。

The Dragon Boat Festival, celebrated on the fifth day of the fifth lunar month, is China's traditional festival. It is also one of Chinese nation's ancient traditional festivals.

节日起源
Festival Origin

关于端午节的由来，纪念屈原之说影响最广、最深。屈原是战国时期楚怀王的大臣，他倡导举贤授能、富国强兵，力主联齐抗秦，但遭到强烈反对，被流放到沅、湘流域，在流放中，他写下了忧国忧民的不朽诗篇。公元前 278 年，秦军攻破楚国郢都，屈原于农历五月初五抱石投汨罗江殉国。屈原的爱国精神和感人诗词深入人心，人们"惜而哀之，世论其辞，以相传焉"，于是在端午节举行各种各样的纪念活动表达对屈原的思念和敬意。

The origin of the Dragon Boat Festival is most widely known for commemorating Qu Yuan, once a minister to King Huai of Chu during the Warring States Period. He advocated

for promoting talented individuals, strengthening the country, and forming alliances against the state of Qin. However, his proposals met with strong oppositions and he was exiled to the regions along the Yuanjiang and Xiangjiang rivers, where he composed immortal poems expressing his concerns for the country and its people. In 278 BCE, the Qin army overtook the capital city—Yingdu of Chu, and Qu threw himself into the Miluo River on May 5th in the lunar calender, sacrificing his life for his country. Qu's patriotic and poignant verses deeply touched the people. So they cherished and mourned him, passing down his legacy through various activities during the Dragon Boat Festival.

节日习俗
Festival Customs

赛龙舟是端午节的主要习俗。据传，古时楚国人舍不得屈原投江，许多人便划船追赶去救他，他们争先恐后，追至洞庭湖却不见屈原的踪迹。之后人们在每年的农历五月初五划龙舟以纪念之。也有传说说屈原投江后，沿江百姓纷纷引舟竞渡前去打捞，并借划龙舟驱散江中鱼虾，以免鱼虾蚕食屈原的身体。后来，赛龙舟成为端午节最普遍的活动之一。1980年赛龙舟被列入中国国家体育比赛项目，1991年以来湖南定期举办国际龙舟节。赛龙舟已经由一项中国传统民间活动变成国际性的体育赛事和文化盛事，深受各国人民的喜爱。

Dragon boat race is one key custom during the Dragon Boat Festival. Legend has it that in ancient times, people of the Chu Kingdom desperately tried to save Qu Yuan as he threw himself into the river. They rowed boats, competing to reach him, but upon arriving at Dongting Lake, he was still nowhere to be found. Since then, dragon boat races have been held every year on the fifth day of the fifth lunar month to commemorate this event. Another version of the legend suggests that after Qu Yuan threw himself into the river, the local people rushed to rescue him by racing their boats and used dragon boat races to scare away fish and shrimp to prevent them from devouring Qu Yuan's body. Over time, dragon boat racing has become one of the most common and widespread activities during the Dragon Boat Festival. In 1980, dragon boat race was included as a national sports competition in China. And since 1991, Hunan Province has regularly hosted the International Dragon Boat Festival. Dragon boat race has evolved from a traditional Chinese folk activity to an international sports event and cultural spectacle, enjoyed by people worldwide.

悬艾叶是端午节的另一个传统习俗。人们在端午节期间会洒扫庭院，将艾条插在门楣上，或悬于堂中，以驱瘟疫和祈求平安；也有人将艾叶制成花环、配饰，佩戴起来用于驱瘴。

Hanging mugwort leaves. Another traditional custom is the hanging of mugwort leaves. People sweep and clean their courtyards, hanging mugwort leaves on door lintels and in their homes to ward off plagues and pray for peace. Some people also make mugwort leaves into flower wreaths or decorative accessories, wearing to ward off diseases.

佩香囊。端午节小孩佩香囊，传说有辟邪驱瘟之意。香囊内有朱砂、雄黄、香药，外包以丝布，清香四溢，再用五色丝线缠绕，做成各种形状，点缀、装饰于小孩的衣襟上，玲珑可爱。

Wearing fragrance sachets. Children wear fragrance sachets during the Dragon Boat Festival. Wearing fragrance sachets can ward off evil spirits and diseases according to legends. The sachets contain cinnabar, realgar, and aromatic herbs, and are wrapped in silk cloth, emitting a pleasant fragrance. They are then adorned with colorful silk threads, crafted into various shapes, and worn as accessories by children, adding a charming touch.

节日饮食
Festival Diet

粽子是端午节最具传统特色的食物。人们在端午节这天浸糯米、洗粽叶、包粽子，北方多以红枣为馅，南方则有豆沙、鲜肉、火腿、咸蛋等多种馅料。端午节吃粽子的风俗不仅在中国盛行不衰，而且流传到了朝鲜、日本及东南亚诸国。

Zongzi, pyramid-shaped dumplings made of glutinous rice and wrapped in bamboo leaves, is the most iconic food of the Dragon Boat Festival. People soak glutinous rice, clean bamboo leaves, and wrap the zongzi themselves. In the northern regions of China, red dates are a popular filling, while in the southern regions, there are various fillings such as bean paste, fresh meat, ham, and salted eggs. The custom of eating zongzi during the Dragon Boat Festival is not only prevalent and enduring in China but has also spread to countries such as the DPRK, Japan, and countries in Southeast Asia.

端午节是中国民间十分盛行的传统节日，寄托了人们迎祥纳福、辟邪除灾的愿望。端午文化在世界上影响广泛，一些国家和地区也开展庆端午活动。

The Dragon Boat Festival is a highly popular traditional folk festival in China. It embodies people's aspirations for welcoming auspiciousness, ushering in good fortune, and warding off evil spirits and disasters. The culture of the Dragon Boat Festival has a widespread influence around the world, with various countries and regions also holding celebrations for the occasion.

七夕节
The Qixi Festival

扫码看视频

在我国，农历七月初七是人们俗称的七夕节，也称为"七巧节""七姐节""女儿节""乞巧节"等，是中国民间的传统节日。

In China, the seventh day of the seventh lunar month is commonly known as the Qixi Festival (Double Seventh Day), or "Qiqiao Festival", "Qijie (Vega) Festival", "Young Girls' Festival", "Begging for Ingenuity Festival", etc. It is a traditional Chinese folk festival.

 **节日起源**
Festival Origin

七夕节的由来最早可以追溯到春秋战国时期，是祭祀牵牛星和织女星的节日。东晋葛洪在《西京杂记》中有"汉彩女常以七月七日穿七孔针于开襟楼，人俱习之"的记载。汉代以后，七夕节与"牛郎织女"的美丽爱情传说联系起来，逐渐成为象征爱情的节日，是古代女子最为重视的日子。

The origin of the Qixi Festival, a festival to worship Altair—Niulang star and Vega—Zhinü star, can be traced back to the Spring and Autumn Period and the Warring States Period. Ge Hong of the Eastern Jin Dynasty wrote in his *Miscellaneous Records of the Western Capital* that "on the seventh day of the seventh lunar month, the palace maids of the Han Dynasty used to thread seven-hole needles on the Kaijin Pavilion (to compete in ingenuity), and then people followed suit." After the Han Dynasty, the Qixi Festival was associated with the touching love legend of Niulang and Zhinü and gradually became a festival symbolizing love, which was the most important day for ancient women.

节日习俗
Festival Customs

穿针乞巧。传说织女心灵手巧，因此古时民间女子在七夕之夜穿针乞巧，祈求自己能像织女一样。

Threading needles and begging for ingenuity. It is said that Zhinü is clever and skillful. So in ancient times, folk women would thread needles at the night of the Qixi Festival, praying for themselves to be like Zhinü.

种生求子是旧时七夕节的习俗。通常在七夕节前几天，人们将绿豆、小麦等种子泡发在碗里，等待发芽之后，在七夕这天用红蓝丝绳将它们束在一起，祈求多子多福。

It is an ancient custom of the Qixi Festival to **plant seeds and beg for fertility**. Usually, people would soak seeds such as mung beans, wheat in a bowl for a few days before the Qixi Festival, and wait until the crops sprout, and then tie them together with red and blue silk ropes on the Qixi Festival in the hope of fertility and fortune.

为牛贺生，又叫"贺牛生日"。为了纪念"牛郎织女"传说中老牛的牺牲精神，儿童会在七夕这一天采摘野花挂在牛角上，以此表达对老牛的尊重。

Celebrating the cattle's birthday. To commemorate the sacrificial spirit of the cattle in the legend of Niulang and Zhinü, children would pick wildflowers and hang them on cattle horns on the Qixi Festival to show their respect.

拜魁星。民间传说农历七月初七是魁星的生日，魁星主掌考运，因此每逢七月初七他的生日，古代读书人都会祭拜魁星。

Worshiping Kuixing (the God of Literature). According to folklore, the seventh day of the seventh lunar month is the birthday of Kuixing, who is in charge of the luck in examinations, so scholars in ancient times will worship Kuixing on this day.

节日饮食
Festival Diet

巧果，又叫"乞巧果子"，主要材料是油、面、糖、蜜，制作时先将白糖放在锅中熔为糖浆，然后和入面粉、芝麻，拌匀后摊在案上擀薄，晾凉后用刀切成长方块，最后折为梭形巧果胚，入油炸至金黄即成。巧果是七夕乞巧的应节食品。

Qiaoguo, is also known as "Qiqiao Pastry". The main ingredients are oil, flour, sugar, and honey. Firstly, sugar is melted into syrup in a pan, and mixed with flour and sesame thoroughly. After cooled down, it is rolled out on a chopping board and cut into rectangular pieces, each of which is finally twisted into a shuttle shape and fried in oil until golden. Qiaoguo is the festival food for the Qixi Festival.

酥糖。在一些地方，七夕这一天糕点铺会制作一些织女形象的酥糖，俗称"巧人""巧酥"，出售时又称为"送巧人"，民间认为吃了这种酥糖的人会变得心灵手巧。

Crunchy candy. In some places, pastry shops will make some crunchy candies in the image of Zhinü, commonly known as "Qiaoren" or "Qiaosu" during the Qixi Festival, while selling candies is also called "Sending Qiaoren". People believe eating these crunchy candies will help them become more intelligent and skillful.

七夕节因被赋予了"牛郎织女"的美丽爱情传说，成为中国最具浪漫色彩的传统节日，部分受中华文化影响的亚洲国家如日本、朝鲜、越南等也会在这一天举行庆祝活动。2006 年 5 月 20 日，七夕节被列入我国第一批国家级非物质文化遗产名录。

The Qixi Festival has become the most romantic traditional festival in China because of the touching love legend of "Niulang and Zhinü". It is also celebrated on this day in some Asian countries affected by Chinese cultures, such as Japan, the DPRK, Vietnam, etc. On May 20, 2006, the Qixi Festival was listed in the first list of the national intangible cultural heritage in China.

中 元 节
The Zhongyuan Festival

扫码看视频

每年的农历七月十五，民间俗称"七月半"或"鬼节"，道教称为"中元节"，佛教称为"盂兰盆节"，是我国重要的传统节日。

The fifteenth day of the seventh lunar month is the day for the Mid-July or China's Ghost Festival, also known as the Zhongyuan Festival among Taoists and Ullambana Festival among Buddhists. It's an important traditional festival in China.

节日起源
Festival Origin

中元节的诞生可追溯到上古时代的祖灵崇拜及相关时祭，传说地官生日是在七月十五日，该日地府会放出全部鬼魂，已故祖先可回家团圆，在这一天民间普遍举行祭

中元节

祀鬼魂的活动。也有"中元"之名起源于魏晋南北朝时期道教的说法，该说法认为自梁代开始，民间仿行印度佛教徒追荐祖先举行"盂兰盆节"，后发展成中元节。

The origin of the Zhongyuan Festival can be traced back to the ancient worship of ancestral spirits and related rituals. According to the legend, the Earth God's birthday falls on the fifteenth day of the seventh lunar month. On this day, the gates of the underworld are opened, allowing all the spirits of the deceased to return home and reunite with their families. It is a common practice for people to offer sacrifices to the spirits of the deceased. The name "Zhongyuan" is said to have originated from the Taoist tradition during the Wei, Jin, and Northern and Southern Dynasties. It is believed that after the Liang Dynasty, folks began to imitate Indian Buddhists in offering sacrifices to ancestors during the Ullambana Festival. This tradition has been passed down and become the Zhongyuan Festival.

节日习俗
Festival Customs

普度。中元节民间部分地区会举行"普度"仪式，重在祭祀孤魂野鬼，与中国传统对祖先鬼魂的崇拜相融合，演变成"祭鬼"，是为了亡者的鬼魂可得救度。

Salvation of souls. During the Zhongyuan Festival, people in some areas will hold rituals of salvation of souls, and provide offerings to the wandering spirits and lonely ghosts. This practice later merged with the traditional Chinese ancestor worship and formed the custom of "ghost worship", with the aim of saving the souls of the deceased.

祭祖。相传中元节祖先也会返家探望子孙，人们传承着以家为单位的祭祖习俗。家家上坟扫墓，祭拜祖先。有的地方也举行接送祖先灵魂的仪式。

Ancestral worship. It is said that during the Zhongyuan Festival, ancestors would return home to visit their descendants. People upheld the custom of ancestor worship within their families. Every family visited the graves of their ancestors and offered sacrifices to commemorate them. In some places, there are also ceremonies to receive and send off the souls of ancestors.

点河灯。中元节最主要的节俗是燃放河灯。河灯的底座大都是用纸板或木板做成莲花形状，或者干脆用莲花叶做底座，因此也叫"荷灯""荷花灯"。人们在荷花灯底座上安放灯盏或蜡烛，在七月十五日夜晚月明风清之际将其放于江河湖水之中，意在为亡者引路。

Floating river lanterns. The main custom of the Zhongyuan Festival is the floating of river lanterns. The base of the river lanterns is mostly made of cardboard or wood and the shape is like a lotus flower. Sometimes it simply uses lotus leaves directly to build the base. Therefore, they are also called "lotus lanterns". People place a lamp or candle on the base and float the lantern in the rivers or lakes on the night of the fifteenth day of the seventh lunar month, hoping to guide the souls of the deceased.

节日饮食
Festival Diet

中元节有的地方会吃鸭，取鸭的谐音"压"，认为吃鸭子庇佑平安。还有的地方会吃濑粉、扁食、饺饼、花馍等。

In some places, people eat duck during the Zhongyuan Festival, as in Chinese, the character "duck" (ya) is homophonous with "suppress" (ya), and it is believed that eating ducks can bless the peace. In other places, people eat rice noodles, wontons, dumplings, flower-shaped steamed buns, and other foods during the festival.

中元节与除夕、清明节、重阳节并称中国传统四大祭祖节日，包含着对故人的思念，其意义在于缅怀祖先，教育后人乐善好施、懂得感恩。

The Zhongyuan Festival, Chinese New Year's Eve, the Qingming Festival, and the Double Ninth Festival, are the four major traditional Chinese ancestral worshiping festivals. The customs of the festivals embody the remembrance of deceased ancestors and emphasize the importance of filial piety towards them. The significance lies in honoring the virtue of ancestors and educating later generations to be generous and grateful.

中 秋 节
The Mid-Autumn Festival

扫码看视频

农历八月十五，是中国民间的传统节日中秋节。在中国的农历里，中秋也称为仲秋，在进入秋季的第二个月，以十五月圆为标志，这天正值三秋之中，故谓之"中秋"。

The 15th day of the eighth lunar month is the traditional Chinese folk festival—Mid-Autumn Festival. In the Chinese lunar calendar, the Mid-Autumn day falls in the second month of autumn, marked by the full moon on the 15th day. Coincided with the middle of the autumn, it is called the "Mid-Autumn Day".

节日起源
Festival Origin

中秋节有悠久的历史。古代帝王有春天祭日、秋天祭月的礼制,《周礼》中就有"中秋"一词的记载。后来,贵族和文人学士纷纷效仿,在中秋时节观赏和祭拜皓月,寄托情怀,这种习俗传到民间后逐渐成为传统活动。到了唐代,中秋节成为官方认定的全国性节日。关于中秋节的传说非常丰富,嫦娥奔月、吴刚伐桂、玉兔捣药之类的神话故事广为流传。

The Mid-Autumn Festival has a long history. The ancient emperors had the ritual system of offering sacrifices to the sun in spring and the moon in autumn, and the phrase "Mid-Autumn Day" was recorded in *The Rites of Zhou*. Later, nobles and literati followed suit, offering sacrifices and expressing their thoughts and feelings under the full, bright moon. After this custom got spread to the grassroots, it gradually became a traditional activity. By the Tang Dynasty (618–907 CE), the Mid-Autumn Festival had become an official national holiday. There're many legends about the Mid-Autumn Festival, among which tales of "Goddess Chang'e Flying to the Moon", "Wu Gang Chopping Trees" and "Moon Rabbit Grinding Herbal Medicine" are widely spread.

节日习俗
Festival Customs

赏月。我国自古就有中秋赏月的习俗。到了周代,每逢中秋夜都要举行迎寒和祭月。在唐代,中秋赏月颇为盛行,中秋咏月也成为唐诗的诸多主题之一。不仅文人学士赏月、咏月,平民百姓亦邀约亲朋好友共同赏月。中秋节设宴赏月的习俗流传至今,人们把酒问月,为美好生活庆贺,为远方亲人祝福,和家人"千里共婵娟"。

Admiring the full moon. Since ancient times, there has been the custom of admiring the full moon on the Mid-Autumn day. In the Zhou Dynasty (1046–256 BCE), people welcomed the beginning of the cold and offered sacrifices to the moon on every Mid-

Autumn night. In the Tang Dynasty, it was very popular to admire the full moon on the Mid-Autumn day, and Mid-Autumn moon became one of the most popular themes of Tang poetry. Not only scholars and literati admired and created work related to the moon, but civilians also invited relatives and friends to enjoy the full moon together. The custom of holding a feast for the Mid-Autumn Festival has been passed on till nowadays. People reflect on the moon while drinking, celebrate the good life, send wishes to the loved ones far away, and "share the beauty she (the moon) displays" with their family though miles apart.

吃月饼。月饼，又叫月团、丰收饼、宫饼、团圆饼等，是古代人们在中秋祭拜月神时用的贡品。南宋时期民间以月饼相赠，取团圆之意，后来人们在中秋赏月和品尝月饼，寓意为家人团圆。今天，月饼的制作越来越精细，馅料多样，外形美观，寄托

着人们思念故乡、思念亲人的情
感和祈盼丰收、幸福的心愿，月
饼也是中秋节赠送亲友、联络感
情的最佳礼品之一。

Eating mooncakes. Mooncake,
also called moon ball, harvest cake,
palace cake, reunion cake, etc., was
an ancient tribute to the God of the
Moon on the Mid-Autumn Festival
in ancient times. In the Southern
Song Dynasty (1127–1279), people gave mooncakes to each other as a symbol of reunion.
Later, people admired the moon and enjoyed mooncakes on the Mid-Autumn Festival, to
mark their family reunion. Today, mooncakes are produced more and more delicately, with
diverse fillings and beautiful appearance, reflecting people's longing for their hometown and
family members, as well as their wish for a good harvest and happiness, and hence become
one of the best gifts for connecting and reaching out to friends and relatives during the Mid-
Autumn Festival.

各地习俗不同。除了赏月、祭月、吃月饼，有的地方盛行中秋节赏桂花，食用桂
花制作的各种食品，以及饮桂花酒。一些地方还形成了特殊的中秋习俗，如江苏的烧
斗香、安徽的堆宝塔、广州的树中秋、晋江的烧塔仔、香港的舞火龙等。

Different customs in different places. In addition to admiring the moon, offering
sacrifices to the moon and eating mooncakes, it is popular to appreciate osmanthus blossoms,
eat various foods made of osmanthus flowers, and drink osmanthus wine in some places
during the Mid-Autumn Festival. Special Mid-Autumn Festival customs have also formed in
some places, such as burning funnel-shaped incense in Jiangsu, building hollow towers with
bricks in Anhui, hanging festive lanterns in Guangzhou, burning cob brick-made towers in
Jinjiang, performing fire dragon dance in Hong Kong and so on.

2006年5月20日，中秋节被国务院列入首批国家级非物质文化遗产名录。2008年
1月1日，中秋节被国务院列为国家法定节假日。

On May 20, 2006, the Mid-Autumn Festival was included in the first batch of national
intangible cultural heritage list by the State Council. On January 1, 2008, the Mid-Autumn
Festival was listed as a national holiday by the State Council.

重 阳 节
The Double Ninth Festival

扫码看视频

重阳节是中国民间传统节日，是每年农历的九月初九。在古代，九是非常尊贵的数字，它和"久"同音，表达了人们希望生命长久、长寿的美好愿望。今天的重阳节被赋予了新的含义，倡导人们重视孝道、懂得感恩、敬老爱老。

The Double Ninth Festival is a traditional Chinese folk holiday, celebrated on the ninth day of the ninth lunar month each year. In ancient times, the number "nine" was a highly revered symbol, as it sounds the same as the Chinese character "久" (pinying jiu, meaning "longevity"), expressing people's wishes for a long and healthy life. Today, the Double Ninth Festival has taken on new significance, advocating people to value filial piety, understand gratitude, and show respect and love towards the elderly.

节日起源
Festival Origin

重阳节源自天象崇拜，可追溯到上古时期，相传重阳为元帝得道之辰。春秋战国时期已有在九月农作物秋收之时祭天帝、祭祖，以谢天帝、祖先恩德的活动，同时还有大型饮宴活动，是由先秦时庆丰收的宴会发展而来的。到了唐代，重阳被正式定为民间的节日，拜神、祭祖及求长寿、饮宴等，构成了重阳节的基本内容。

The Double Ninth Festival, originating from the worship of celestial phenomena, can be traced back to ancient times. Legend has it that the Double Ninth Festival is the day when Emperor Yuan achieved enlightenment. During the Spring and Autumn Period and the Warring States Period, people already held activities in September to offer sacrifices to the Emperor of Heaven and ancestors, to show gratitude for their benevolence during the autumn harvest. At the same time, there were large-scale banquet activities, which had been developed from the harvest banquet in the pre-Qin period. During the Tang Dynasty, the Double Ninth Festival was officially designated as a folk holiday. Worshiping gods and ancestors, praying for longevity, feasting, etc. formed the basic content of the Double Ninth Festival.

节日习俗
Festival Customs

登高。在古代，民间有重阳登高的风俗，故重阳节又叫"登高节"。重阳是"清气上扬、浊气下沉"的时节，地势越高，清气越聚集，于是"重阳登高畅享清气"便成了民俗事项。金秋九月，天高气爽，这个季节登高远望可达到心旷神怡、健身祛病的目的。

Climbing to high places. In ancient times, there was a custom of climbing to high places during the Double Ninth Festival, which is why it is also called the "Climbing Festival". Double Ninth is a time when "clear air rises and turbid air sinks". The higher the location, the more the clear air gathers, so climbing high to enjoy the clear air has become a folk tradition. In the cool and clear weather of September, climbing to high places can achieve the purpose of refreshing the mind, promoting physical fitness, and preventing diseases.

赏菊。重阳节正是一年的金秋时节，此时菊花盛开，人们会赏菊花、饮酒、赋诗等，据传这些都起源于诗人陶渊明，其诗句"采菊东篱下，悠然见南山"流传至今。菊花是中国的名花，具有高洁、质朴的品格，象征长寿，民间还把农历九月称为"菊月"，在菊花怒放的重阳节，观赏菊花成了该节日的一项重要庆祝活动。

Admiring chrysanthemums. The Double Ninth Festival falls in the golden autumn season when chrysanthemums are in full bloom. People enjoy admiring chrysanthemums, drinking wine, and composing poetry. It is said that these originated from the poet Tao Yuanming's famous verse "Picking chrysanthemums by the eastern fence, leisurely seeing the southern mountain", which has been passed down to this day. The chrysanthemum is a famous flower in China, representing purity, simplicity, and longevity. The Chinese lunar calendar's ninth month is also known as "Chrysanthemum Month". Admiring chrysanthemums during the Double Ninth Festival has become an important part of the holiday festivities.

饮菊花酒。菊花酒在古代被看作重阳必饮、祛灾祈福的"吉祥酒"。饮菊花酒在汉魏时期就已经开始盛行。人们在菊花盛开之时，采集菊花的茎叶，与谷物掺在一起酿酒，等到来年农历九月九日饮用。

Drinking chrysanthemum wine. Chrysanthemum wine was considered an "auspicious wine" that must be consumed during the Double Ninth Festival in ancient times, believed to bring blessing and ward off disasters. Its popularity dates back to the Han and Wei dynasties.

People usually gather chrysanthemum stems and leaves when they are in full bloom, mix them with grains to ferment wine, and then drink it on the ninth day of the ninth lunar month in the following year.

插茱萸。重阳节有插茱萸的风俗，古人认为在重阳节这一天插茱萸能够祛除疾病、辟邪消灾。因此很多人会在重阳节这天登高采茱萸，将茱萸插在门前，或者做成香囊佩戴于手臂上，也有把茱萸放在香袋里面佩戴的，多为妇女和儿童。

Inserting dogwood. The Double Ninth Festival is celebrated with the custom of inserting dogwood. Ancient people believed that inserting dogwood on this day could ward off diseases, and avoid evil and disasters. Therefore, many people would climb up high to collect dogwood on the Double Ninth Festival, insert it in front of their doors, or make it into sachets to wear on their arms. Some women and children also wear dogwood in their sachets.

节日饮食
Festival Diet

吃重阳糕。重阳糕又称花糕、菊糕、五色糕，制无定法，较为随意。重阳节敬老，登高以避灾。"糕"与"高"同音，有"步步高升""寿高九九"的含义，所以"重阳花糕"成了最受欢迎的节日食品之一。

Eating Chongyang Cake. Chongyang Cake, also known as Flower Cake, Chrysanthemum Cake, or Five-color Cake, has no fixed recipe and is made in a more casual manner. The Double Ninth Festival is a day to respect the elderly and climb high to avoid disasters. The Chinese character "糕" (cake) sounds similar to "高" (high) in Chinese, and it carries the meaning of "rising step by step" and "longevity reaching ninety-nine". Therefore, "Chongyang Flower Cake" has become one of the most popular festive foods.

吃螃蟹。秋风起，蟹脚痒，陈酒醇，桂花香。秋季是螃蟹最肥美的季节，螃蟹是重阳节的应季食物，是人们喜爱的美食之一。

Eating crab. Autumn wind blows, crab feet itch, aged wine is mellow, and osmanthus fragrance permeates. Autumn is the season when crabs are the most delicious. Crabs are a seasonal food for the Double Ninth Festival and one of the favorite cuisines that people love to eat.

人们在重阳节用敬祖、尊老、敬老行为体现敬老孝亲和慎终追远等中华民族的优良传统。

重阳节

During the Double Ninth Festival, people demonstrate the traditional Chinese nation's best traditions of cultivating respect for the dead and carrying the memory back to the distant past by respecting ancestors, respecting and caring for the elderly.

腊 八 节
The Laba Festival

扫码看视频

腊八节又称"腊八祭""腊日祭""王侯腊""佛成道日",节期在每年农历十二月初八。

The Laba Festival is also called "Laba Ji" "Lari Ji" "Wanghou La" and known as "Buddha's Enlightenment Day" in Chinese Buddhism. It falls on the eighth day of the twelfth lunar month every year.

节日起源
Festival Origin

腊八节原来是古代欢庆丰收、感谢祖先和神灵的祭祀仪式,夏朝称腊为"嘉平",商朝称之为"清祀",周朝称之为"大蜡",因在十二月举行,故称该月为腊月,称腊祭这一天为腊日。先秦的腊日在冬至后的第三个戌日,正如《说文解字》记载:"冬至后三戌,腊祭百神。"自南北朝开始,腊日固定在腊月初八。

The Laba Festival was originally an ancient sacrificial ceremony to celebrate the harvest, where people expressed gratitude to ancestors and gods. It's called "Jiaping" in the Xia Dynasty, "Qingsi" in the Shang Dynasty and "Dala (big wax)" in the Zhou Dynasty. As it was held in the twelfth month, this month was called "Layue". And the day of the ceremony was called "Lari". In the pre-Qin period, "Lari" was set on the third Xu (戌) Day after Winter Solstice. As recorded in *Origin of Chinese Characters*, "The third Xu Day after Winter Solstice is the time to offer sacrifices to all the gods." Since the beginning of the Northern and Southern Dynasties, "Lari" was fixed on the eighth day of the twelfth lunar month.

腊八节后来演化成纪念佛祖释迦牟尼成道的宗教节日。据传,佛教创始人释迦牟尼在深山修行,静坐六年,饿得骨瘦如柴,曾欲弃此苦,恰遇一牧羊女,送他乳糜,他食罢盘腿坐于菩提树下,于十二月初八之日悟道成佛,从此佛门定此日为"佛成道日"。因与腊日融合,就成为腊八节,人们在这一天举行隆重的礼仪活动。

The Laba Festival later developed into a religious festival commemorating Buddha Sakyamuni's enlightenment. Legend has it that Shakyamuni, the founder of Buddhism, practiced reclusively in the deep mountains, and was very hungry and skinny after six years of seated meditation. He was almost about to give up when he just met a shepherdess, who gave him some semi-fluid mass of diary, he ate it and sat cross-legged under a Bodhi tree and enlightened into Buddha on the eighth day of the twelfth lunar month, hence the day of Buddha's Enlightenment Day in Chinese Buddhism. It was then celebrated together with the "Lari", and became the Laba Festival, when grand ceremonial activities were held.

节日习俗
Festival Customs

老北京流传着这样一首民谣，头两句是"小孩小孩你别馋，过了腊八就是年"。腊八节拉开了过年的序幕，许多人家开始采购年货，"年"的气氛逐渐浓厚。

There is a folk song in old Beijing that begins with, "Don't be greedy, children, after the Laba comes the New Year." The Laba Festival opens the prelude to the Lunar New Year. Many people begin to purchase New Year goods. The atmosphere for the New Year becomes stronger and stronger.

喝腊八粥。作为佛教盛大的节日之一，腊八节这天，各寺院举行法会，参照佛陀成道前牧女献乳糜的典故，用谷物和水果等煮粥供佛，名为腊八粥。传说喝了这种粥以后，就可以得到佛祖的保佑，因此，腊八粥也叫"福寿粥""福德粥""佛粥"。最早的腊八粥是煮红小豆，后经演变，加之地方特色，腊八粥形式逐渐丰富起来。

Eating Laba porridge. As one of the grand festivals of Buddhism, monasteries will

perform rituals on the Laba Festival. Sharing the spirit of the legendary shepherdess, monasteries will offer porridge made of grains and fruits, called the Laba porridge. It's said that those who have the auspicious Laba porridge will get the blessing from the Buddha. Therefore, Laba porridge is also called "Fu Shou (blessing and longevity) porridge", "Fu De (blessing and virtues) porridge" or "Buddha porridge". Originally, the Laba porridge was made of red beans, and gradually became rich and colorful with local characteristics.

泡腊八蒜。在腊八节这天，北方尤其是华北地区流行泡腊八蒜。人们将剥了皮的蒜瓣儿放到一个可以密封的罐子里，然后倒入醋，封上口，放到一个温度较低的地方。慢慢地，泡在醋里的蒜就会变绿，最后会变得通体碧绿，如同翡翠。

Pickling Laba garlic. On the day of the Laba Festival, it is popular in the north, especially in North China, to make Laba garlic, a kind of pickled garlic. Put the peeled garlic into a jar that can be sealed, pour in the vinegar, seal the jar, and put it in a place with low temperature. Slowly, the garlic soaked in vinegar will turn green, and finally the whole body of the garlic will be as green as jade.

吃腊八面。腊八面是流行于陕西关中地区腊八节的传统面食。在陕西省渭北一带的澄城地区，当地人在腊八节一般是不喝粥的。在每年农历腊月初八的早上，家家户户都要吃用各种果蔬做臊子的腊八面。

Eating Laba noodles. Laba noodles are a traditional pasta dish popular for the Laba Festival in the Guanzhong region in central Shaanxi Province. In the Chengcheng region of Weibei area in Shaanxi, porridge is not the signature food for the Laba Festival. In the morning of this day, people usually have noodle soup topped with various sliced vegetables.

中国的传统节日总是内敛而含蓄的，一般是家人之间的其乐融融，但腊八节似乎走出了家人的小圈子。人们通过馈赠与接受腊八粥，在社会中与他人建立了更广泛的情感联系，体现了中华民族血脉深处济世为民的高尚情怀和广阔胸襟。

Traditional Chinese festivals are always reserved and implicit in emotions, generally about sharing joy among family members. But the Laba Festival seems to be different, when people go out of their small circle of family and kins to build wider connections with others and the society by giving and receiving porridge. It also reflects the virtue of helping and serving people for the well-being of the society, which runs deep in the blood of the Chinese people.

祭 灶 节

The Kitchen God Festival

扫码看视频

　　春节是中华民族最盛大的传统佳节，俗称过大年。祭灶节又称小年，大约在春节前一周。中国北方的大部分地区在腊月二十三过小年，南方则在腊月二十四过小年。以下以腊月二十三作为小年进行介绍。

　　The Spring Festival is the most celebrated traditional festival of the Chinese nation, commonly known as the Chinese New Year. The Kitchen God Festival, or Xiaonian, falls on about a week before the Chinese New Year. The 23rd day of the 12th lunar month is known as Xiaonian in most parts of northern China, while in the south Xiaonian is celebrated on the 24th. Here, we will introduce Xiaonian on the 23rd day of the 12th lunar month.

节日起源
Festival Origin

　　旧时，差不多每家的灶间都设有"灶王爷"的神位，人们称这尊神为"灶君司命"，传说他负责管理各家的灶火，被当作一家的保护神而受到祭拜。灶王爷自上一年的除夕以来就一直留在家中履行保护和监察职责，到了腊月二十三日，便升上天去向玉皇大帝汇报这一家人的善行或恶行。玉皇大帝根据灶王爷的汇报，将这一家在新的一年中应该得到的吉凶祸福交到灶王爷手中。因此，一家人往往举行送灶仪式，请灶王爷对玉皇大帝进"好言"，于是就形成了腊月二十三给灶王爷上供、祈求合家平安的习俗。自周朝开始，皇宫将祭灶列入祭典，在全国立下祭灶的规矩，祭灶就成为固定的仪式了。

　　In the old days, almost every household had a shrine for the Kitchen God, revered as "the Kitchen God of Life and Death". Legend has it that the Kitchen God is a deity responsible for managing the fireplaces in households and ensuring the safety of families. The Kitchen God had been staying at home since the previous Lunar New Year's Eve to perform his duties of protection and supervision. And on the 23rd day of the 12th lunar month, he ascended to heaven to report the good or bad deeds of the family to the Jade Emperor, the Supreme Deity of Taoism. According to the report of the Kitchen God, the Jade Emperor would entrust the family's fortune and misfortune for the upcoming year to the Kitchen God. Therefore, the

family would hold a ceremony to bid farewell to the Kitchen God, asking him to put in a good word for them to the Jade Emperor. This has formed the tradition of offering sacrifices to the Kitchen God, and praying for the peace and safety of the whole family on the 23rd day of the 12th lunar month. Since the Zhou Dynasty, the imperial palace included the offering to the Kitchen God in the sacrificial rites, making it a fixed ceremony.

节日习俗
Festival Customs

送灶，也称"辞灶"，多在黄昏入夜之时举行。一家人在灶房摆上桌子，向设在灶壁神龛中的灶王爷敬香，并供上用饴糖和面做成的糖瓜等。

Bidding farewell to the Kitchen God. It is mostly held at dusk or during the evening. The family sets up a table in the kitchen, offering incense to the Kitchen God in a shrine on the kitchen wall, and serving Tanggua, a melon-shaped candy made of malt sugar and flour.

放鞭炮。腊月二十三这天晚上，人们会放鞭炮，意为送灶神。

Setting off firecrackers. On the evening of the 23rd day of the 12th lunar month, people will set off firecrackers, as a way to send off the Kitchen God.

扫尘。祭灶后便正式开始为迎接新年做准备了，民间把每年腊月二十三日至除夕的这段时间叫作"迎春日"或"扫尘日"。扫尘就是年终大扫除，各家各户都要认真彻底地进行清扫，做到窗明几净，这一习俗寄托着人们辞旧迎新的愿望和祈求。

Sweeping dust. After the sacrifice, people officially start preparing for the New Year. This period from the 23rd day of the 12th lunar month to the New Year's Eve is called "Spring-welcoming Day" or "Dust-sweeping Day". During this year-ending period, every household will conscientiously clean and tidy up, ensuring that the windows and furniture are clean and bright. This practice embodies people's wishes for ushering in the New Year and bidding farewell to the old.

节日饮食
Festival Diet

吃饺子。北方小年晚上习惯吃饺子，意为给灶王爷送行，取意"送行饺子迎风面"。

Eating dumplings. This is a tradition in northern China on the evening of Xiaonian to bid farewell to the Kitchen God and welcome a new year, following the custom of "sending off someone with dumplings and welcoming with noodles".

吃灶糖。灶糖是祭灶节的传统食物，是一种很黏的麦芽糖。把它抻成长条形的糖棍，就是"关东糖"，把它抟成扁圆形，就叫作"糖瓜"。

Eating malt sugar. The sticky malt sugar is an iconic food for the Kitchen God Festival. When it is pulled into the long strip form, it is called "Guandong candy", and when it is shaped into flat rounds, it is called "melon-shaped candy".

炒玉米。晋东南地区，有吃炒玉米的习俗，民谣有"二十三，不吃炒，大年初一——锅倒"的说法。人们喜欢把炒的玉米用麦芽糖粘起来，再冻成大块，吃起来酥脆香甜。

Stir-frying corn. In the southeast of Shanxi Province, there is a custom of eating fried corn. A folk saying goes, "If you don't eat stir-fried corn on the 23rd day, you will spill the entire pot on New Year's Day." People like to combine stir-fried corn with maltose to make it crispy and sweet, and freeze it into large pieces for consumption.

祭灶是我国民间影响很大、流传很广的一个习俗，它拉开了春节的序幕。

Offering sacrifices to the Kitchen God is a widely practiced and influential folk custom in China, marking the start of the Chinese New Year.

后 记

　　在经历了无数个日夜的辛勤笔耕、视频创作之后，《文化里的中国》终于要与读者们见面了，这是我负责的国家民委"道中华"双语文化传播工作室的成果，是我主持的校级重点科研项目"增强中华文化传播力影响力路径研究"（项目编号：2023SHKX15）的成果，是我们北方民族大学师生组成的这个团队献给学校40周年校庆的一份礼物，也是我们团队共同成长的见证。

　　本书源于2021年10月我发起创建的旨在"用英语传播中国声音、讲好中国故事"的校级学生社团——北方民族大学华韵文化双语传播社。社团成立之初，我指导杨雨琪、杨书鹏、吴经纬、王子怡、何煜晖、苏晓康、祁炎爽、刘家彤等社团骨干进行创作，逐渐形成了成语故事、民间故事、神话故事、中国古诗词、二十四节气和习语习典六大系列作品，并创建了同名视频号，自2022年3月8日起，以每周一期的更新速度，发布原创的双语视频。

　　2023年，我先后邀请了外国语学院教师吴坤和杜娟、马克思主义学院教师谭月娥、电气信息工程学院教师丁黎明、设计艺术学院教师陈晨加入团队，在校内跨学院组建了一支稳定的师生创作团队，并于4月13日获批成立国家民委"道中华"双语文化传播工作室，旨在深入学习贯彻习近平新时代中国特色社会主义思想和党的二十大精神，围绕铸牢中华民族共同体意识工作主线，充分发挥国际传播中的语言优势，依托原创短视频作品，用汉英双语传播中华优秀传统文化。工作室创作的大量原创作品深受读者喜爱，被国家民委"道中华"公众号、外媒平台（Facebook、YouTube、Instagram、Twitter）、中国驻旧金山总领事馆等转载。

我们团队始终以"讲好中国故事、传播好中国声音，展现可信、可爱、可敬的中国形象"为目标，在两年多的时间里围绕二十四节气、中国古诗词、传统节日、中国传统故事创作了系列原创作品。为确保文本质量，所有文稿均经过多次审校，英文翻译选择业内认可度高的学者的翻译，如"诗词里的中国"系列作品的翻译选自被誉为"诗译英法唯一人"的北京大学教授、翻译家许渊冲先生，并获得了许先生嫡亲弟子崔秀娟女士的支持。为了让这些作品被更多人看到，我们边创作边整理，形成了《文化里的中国》视频书，以中英双语来展示，并配有原创插图和视频作品二维码，实现了"书中有视频，视频印书中"，将中华优秀传统文化的内宣和外宣结合起来。

在《文化里的中国》出版之际，我要感谢学校给予我们的大力支持，校党委书记、校长李俊杰教授百忙之中为本书作序，其他校领导也大力支持本书出版，校庆办、校友会、科研处、校党委宣传部、中华民族共同体处、校团委、外国语学院等部门也给予了大力支持和帮助。我要感谢中国人民大学出版社编辑的辛苦付出，是你们的严谨和专业，才使这本书得以顺利出版。我要感谢中国新闻网海外版、国家民委"道中华"视频号以及其他媒体平台对我们作品的认可以及对其进行发布与宣传，尤其要感谢中国新闻网海外中心的冯爽、陈天浩、吴辛茹等编辑一直以来对工作室作品严格把关，使我们的作品顺利在海外媒体发布，并被转载。我要感谢在预览本书文稿后给予肯定、支持与推荐的中央民族大学教授蒙曼、宁夏作协主席郭文斌、许渊冲先生嫡亲弟子崔秀娟等。同时，我也要感谢我的团队成员、所有为这本书付出辛勤劳动的社团学生，尤其是苏晓康、奈峥、吴经纬在书稿的英文校对，刘朝翔在书稿的配图，田文慧和李祉仪等在视频制作方面的付出，杨书鹏、王子怡、何煜晖等在视频配音及演绎等方面的付出。没有你们的鼎力支持，这本书无法如期并高质量地呈现在读者面前。

最后，我想对读者朋友们说：愿这本书能够陪伴你们度过一段美好的时光，如书中有不足之处还请批评指正，希望我们一起传播好中国声音，讲好中国故事！

谨以此书献给北方民族大学，愿其四十载春华秋实，继往开来，再创辉煌！

北方民族大学

张玫

2024 年 7 月

图书在版编目（CIP）数据

文化里的中国：汉文、英文 / 张玫等编著；陈晨
配图.––北京：中国人民大学出版社，2024.8.
ISBN 978-7-300-33132-4

Ⅰ. K203
中国国家版本馆 CIP 数据核字第 2024VW2845 号

文化里的中国

编　著　张　玫　谭月娥　杜　娟　吴　坤　丁黎明
配　图　陈　晨
Wenhua Li de Zhongguo

出版发行	中国人民大学出版社	
社　　址	北京中关村大街 31 号	邮政编码　100080
电　　话	010-62511242（总编室）	010-62511770（质管部）
	010-82501766（邮购部）	010-62514148（门市部）
	010-62515195（发行公司）	010-62515275（盗版举报）
网　　址	http://www.crup.com.cn	
经　　销	新华书店	
印　　刷	涿州市星河印刷有限公司	
开　　本	787 mm×1092 mm　1/16	版　　次　2024 年 8 月第 1 版
印　　张	13.25	印　　次　2025 年 3 月第 2 次印刷
字　　数	257 000	定　　价　98.00 元

中国人民大学出版社读者信息反馈表

尊敬的读者：

感谢您购买和使用中国人民大学出版社的 _____ 一书，我们希望通过这张小小的反馈表来获得您更多的建议和意见，以改进我们的工作，加强我们双方的沟通和联系。我们期待着能为更多的读者提供更多的好书。

请您填妥下表后，寄回或传真回复我们，对您的支持我们不胜感激！

1. 您是从何种途径得知本书的：
   □书店　　　　□网上　　　　□报纸杂志　　　　□朋友推荐

2. 您为什么决定购买本书：
   □工作需要　　□学习参考　　□对本书主题感兴趣　　□随便翻翻

3. 您对本书内容的评价是：
   □很好　　　　□好　　　　□一般　　　　□差　　　　□很差

4. 您在阅读本书的过程中有没有发现明显的专业及编校错误，如果有，它们是：

   _____

   _____

   _____

5. 您对哪些专业的图书信息比较感兴趣：

   _____

   _____

6. 如果方便，请提供您的个人信息，以便于我们和您联系（您的个人资料我们将严格保密）：

   您供职的单位：_____

   您教授的课程（教师填写）：_____

   您的通信地址：_____

   您的电子邮箱：_____

请联系我们：黄婷　程子殊　王新文　王琼

电话：010-62512737，62513265，62515580，62515573

传真：010-62514961

E-mail：huangt@crup.com.cn　　chengzsh@crup.com.cn　　wangxw@crup.com.cn
　　　　 crup_wy@163.com

通信地址：北京市海淀区中关村大街甲59号文化大厦15层　　　邮编：100872

中国人民大学出版社